COLOR
FOR WEBSITES

Molly E. Holzschlag

Published and distributed
by RotoVision SA

Rue du Bugnon 7
CH-1299 Crans-Près-Céligny
Switzerland

RotoVision SA
Sales, Production & Editorial Office
Sheridan House, 112–116A Western Road
Hove, East Sussex, BN3 1DD, UK

TEL   +44 (0)1273 72 72 68
FAX   +44 (0)1273 72 72 69

        sales@rotovision.com
        www.rotovision.com

ISBN 2-88046-542-7

10   9   8

7   6   5

4   3   2

1

Design by
Public, San Francisco

Production and separations by
ProVision Pte. Ltd., Singapore

TEL   +65 334 7720
FAX   +65 334 7721

Most of the illustrations
and paintings in this book
were provided courtesy
of artist Joe Forkan,
http://www.joeforkan.com/.

Most of the original
photographs in this book
were provided courtesy
of photographer Derrick Story,
http://www.storyphoto.com/.

PP 38–39
© 2000 Sky Bergman
http://www.skybergman.com/.

PP 54–55
Courtesy Cesar Rubio
http://www.cesarrubio.com/.

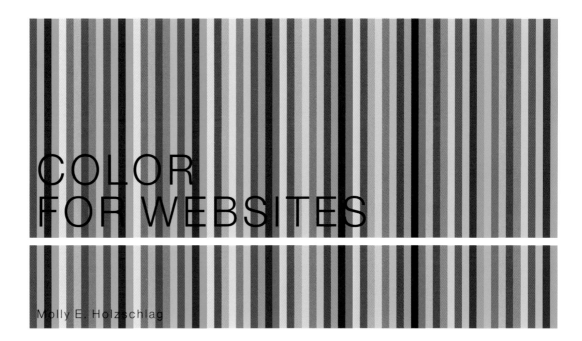

COLOR
FOR WEBSITES

Molly E. Holzschlag

RotoVision

Acknowledgements

I'd like to thank the following people for their contributions to this book: My editor, Natalia Price-Cabrera—RotoVision's Editor-in-Chief—who took such kind care to work with me through the difficult spots. Todd Foreman and his assistant Tessa Lee who made my words come to life with the book's visual design.

Joseph Forkan very generously allowed me to use his cartoons, illustrations, and paintings to enhance this book. Visit Joe's site at www.joeforkan.com. Derrick Story spiritedly provided awesome photography for the book. Derrick's site is at www.storyphoto.com. Please visit both for these exceptional friends and thank them for sharing their talent and vision! Wanda Cummings provided wonderful materials to inspire and guide. J. L. Morton is always brilliant. And thank you to Sky Bergman and Cesar Rubio who kindly contributed photographic material too.

To all my friends and family, thank you for coloring my world.

Table of Contents

Introduction

Color serves to entice, seduce, frighten, excite, empower, and soothe. Name any human emotion, and there is a color to go with it. In fact, our language includes countless references to color as emotion:

"Bob's in a red rage."

"Camilla is feeling blue."

"I'm in the pink."

"Mary's green with envy."

That emotion and color are so strongly connected is simply a product of nature. The very fact that humans have the ability to perceive color (although indeed, there are many who cannot, or cannot do so correctly) suggests that we've evolved to a point where color cues in nature are necessary parts of our survival abilities. In our sophisticated world, we've used this as a means to assist communication: red means stop, green means go, yellow means caution.

Designers who are academically trained are often exposed to color theory as well as the psychological and international perceptions of color. However, the independent spirit of the Web has given rise to many instances where people with no formal training in design are finding themselves responsible for esthetic decisions. Some people have an innate sense of color, but many do not. There's a good argument to be made that most people designing for the Web are in fact visual illiterates. They do not understand how to effectively use space, shape, type, or color to create designs that are both appropriate to the audiences they serve, and the purpose for which they exist.

Because of this, a book on Web color makes a great deal of sense. First, there are numerous technology issues I cover that both Web newcomers and very experienced designers will find of benefit. I'll begin with a look at organic versus digital color, describe color relationships, effects and properties, and review color models in use for the digital designer. Once these standard color principles are under your belt, I move on to show you how to use these principles in the context of the Web. I discuss technical considerations, color for browsers, designing across browsers and platforms, and how to specify color using Web mark-up. Case studies and design samples provide real-world representations of how color comes to life within the context of the Web.

Of course, color extends to images, so a portion of this book is dedicated to helping you make expert decisions as to file formats, and how to process those files to retain the utmost color integrity. I'll examine special technical options found in various formats, and provide plenty of samples of successful, and unsuccessful, use of Web graphic technology.

But more importantly, at least in my way of thinking, is that along with any study of technology must also co-exist theoretical principles, which challenge the mind and serve the creative muse.

Color theory comprises the visual as well as the psychological. I'll examine the way color comes (if you'll pardon the obvious pun) to light. But I'll also spend plenty of time focusing on the reasons why you'll want to use a specific color, or set of colors (or not) in a given circumstance. The psychological impact of color is something that only a few select scholars have spent time investigating. Yet, it is the heart and soul of color design. A designer who understands which color to use to convey a specific meaning; what combination of colors can relax a website visitor or help sell a product; or which colors can upset or anger, is a designer who is empowered.

Perhaps most interesting in terms of color's psychological impact is the way color works in a global setting. If you're designing for the Web, it's important to remember that this medium is, after all, worldwide. As such, the differences in color perception become extremely important. Why is blue a very safe color globally? Which colors are necessary to avoid in certain countries? This book will answer such questions, and provide insight into the often paradoxical meanings that are inherent to color across nations.

Finally, I provide a library of color swatches that you can use to guide you in your color design endeavors. These samples are sophisticated color schemes that will serve to help you explore ideas as well as serve your Web audiences effectively.

And, while this book will give you techniques and provide concepts, it is also intended to be a visual inspiration. The art, photography, websites, and actual design of the book have all been chosen with utmost care to ensure that the experience of this book directly correlates to its technical and creative goals: to educate, to inspire, and to beautify the Web, and the world.

COLOR
FOUNDATIONS

Chapter One

natural and digital

. . . how color is seen and interpreted in the real world is very different from the way
we see color on a computer screen, and gaining insight into these differences will inspire
you as a Web designer to create designs that can draw from the esthetic beauty
of the world around you as well as take advantage of the strengths of the digital world.

The physical perception of color is, for the person who has accurate, healthy color vision, a process by which light illuminates an object and is interpreted by the person.

The process by which this interpretation occurs is only partially understood by scientists. What we do know is that within the retina we have cones and rods that respond to hues and brightness—with the cones having the ability to respond to hues and light, but the rods only responding to light. This information is in turn transmitted to our brains, which process and interpret the light's play on a given object as a color.

If this process sounds complicated, it is. And, since all people are different, the ultimate perception of color is likely to be different as well. This means that color is by and large subjective.

How we as Web designers capture this complex and subjective process begins with our ability to understand the history and mechanisms by which scientists and artists have agreed to describe color. This study is referred to as *Color Theory*. What's more, how color is seen and interpreted in the real world is very different from the way we see color on a computer screen, and gaining insight into these differences will inspire you as a Web designer to create designs that can draw from the esthetic beauty of the world around you as well as take advantage of the strengths of the digital world.

Colors also have relationships, and the interplay of colors within these relationships can create effects. Harnessing the power of these relationships and interplay allows the Web designer to create designs that are appropriate for their goals and in turn create successful sites. Understanding the way color is technically organized provides a strong foundation when working with digital color, particularly when dealing with websites.

It's important to remember that not all people have the capacity to see color at all, or to see it correctly. Color blindness is considered to be relatively common in men, with 6–8% of all men having some deficiency in color perception. Interestingly enough, very few women suffer from color blindness.

Organic and Digital Color

What do you think of when you hear the word "organic?" Do you think of Birkenstock-wearing, University of California Berkeley grad students eating sprout-laden salads and doing yoga? Maybe you think of expensive—but clean—produce. The word organic has a lot of odd connotations, but it simply means "of or derived from a living organism." Conceivably, organic is anything that is or was once in part alive.

When I was a child growing up in New Jersey, I used to spend countless hours in my backyard digging in the dirt. While most people think of New Jersey as a highly industrialized state, it is also a very fecund place. So much so that it is referred to as the Garden State. Its soil is rich and varied and it produces some of the most delicious produce and rolling fields of wildflowers anywhere.

To my young senses, the earth was an especially awesome place. Its colors were variegated—rich browns were tempered by sandy stretches. In the spring it was alive with flowers, vegetables, and fruits of bright jewel tones. In the summer, its long grasses would turn golden with the sun's influence. And upon the earth a rich and colorful world of its own: earthworms in huge coffee-colored clumps of swarming life, white and speckled rabbits, red foxes, blue and red birds.

The organic world—the live world—is awash with color. Take some time to go outside and look around.

Sometimes the color is bright, and sometimes it's muted. Perhaps you're in a city, and it's raining. Or maybe you're in the country, at dawn. The colors move you, don't they? Whether bright or muted, we respond emotionally to color.

The colors in nature are where we find our inspiration for the work we as designers do in the digital world. While the two are vastly different worlds—they are intractably connected. Your ability to experience color in its natural state is necessary for you to effectively express color as a Web designer working in the digital world.

In fact, the connection between what is organic and what is digital creates a compelling argument as to whether or not digital is an extension of the organic or is something that exists outside of organic matter. While computers are made of plastic, silicon—a lot of fabricated materials—they are inspired and influenced in part by what is organic. And of course, they mean nothing without the input from us as people. So the argument can be made that the digital world is of, and derived from, a living organism.

I personally like to think there is no separation between the organic and digital worlds, at least at their essence, or from a philosophical perspective. But when we look to the technical realities of how color is created and perceived, there do exist differences. Knowing these differences is imperative to the color designer. He or she must understand why color that is expressed in paint, dye, or ink is different from color that is expressed on a computer screen. What's more, the history of organic color is much, much older than that of digital, and as such is much more consistent.

The work of many philosophers, artists, and scientists has culminated in an awareness that color, in its organic form, is viewed by the human eye in a process that involves the perception of light. Color and light are inseparable.

Subtractive Color

From nature—from the roots of plants, the leaves of trees, the skins of fruit—we extract dyes that enable us to create expressions of natural color in an interpretive sense. The need to express in color—and to understand color—is as old as human history.

Many great thinkers throughout time have studied color, determined to understand what it is, why it is, and why it has such profound influence on the human psyche. From Pythagoras, who described color in terms of music, and Da Vinci, who formulated theories on the mixing of paints that led to the understanding of primary and secondary colors, to Sir Isaac Newton's take on a more circular system of linked colors; our history is filled with great minds who reached for an understanding of what color is, what its properties are, and perhaps most importantly: what color *means*.

The work of many philosophers, artists, and scientists has culminated in an awareness that color, in its organic form, is viewed by the human eye in a process that involves the perception of light. Color and light are inseparable. Without light, color would be imperceptible. And, because of light, color is possible in both the organic and digital worlds.

The process by which the human eye perceives color is referred to as *subtractive synthesis*. A subtractive color absorbs, reflects, and transmits light. In turn, our eyes perceive that light as color. Whether we're looking at a plant, a fish, a bird—or dyes, pigments, and inks—this synthesis forms the basis for all color in the organic world.

Subtractive color begins with what has now been classified as *primary* colors: red, yellow, and blue (see Figure 1.1). All colors in or derived from nature are either these colors or some combination of these colors. By mixing pairs of primary colors together, we come up with *secondary* colors. And, by mixing two primaries in a ratio of 2:1, we get *intermediate* (also known as *tertiary*) colors. White is pure reflective light, and black is the absence of light.

The important thing to remember about subtractive synthesis is that while we add one pigment to another to get another color, the process by which the color is perceived has to do with the perception of that color's absorption of light—which is a subtractive, not additive process.

1.1

Primary colors
in subtractive synthesis:
red, yellow, and blue

Additive Color

While I can take paint and mix it together to create another pigment that, along with subtractive synthesis, enables us to see color, I can't do this within a computer's depths. In order to achieve color in the digital world, light stimulus must be added to other light in order to create color. This process is referred to as *additive synthesis*. In this model, the primary colors most commonly at work are red, green, and blue (Figure 1.2).

A perfect example of additive synthesis is your television screen. When you look at the picture on a TV screen, you're really looking at thousands of phosphor dots made up of red, green, and blue. The dots are tiny, so they appear to blend together to achieve a given color. RGB computer monitors work the same way (Figure 1.3).

Additive color originates within an algorithm that numerically determines how much of a given light stimulus makes up the color in question.

Each individual color available on a computer contains some percentage of red, green, or blue. So, with a computer, I can mix a bit of red light, a bit of blue light, and a bit of green light and come up with yellow light.

Specifically, secondary colors in the additive process are created using the same ratio as is found in subtractive synthesis. Therefore, if I mix one part of red with one part of blue, I get a secondary color—in this case, magenta.

The absence of light stimulus makes black, and the equal portions of each red, blue, and green make up white.

Switch back to the subtractive process for a moment: If I mixed red, blue, and green pigment in equal amounts I'd end up with brown. On the other hand, if I mix red, blue, and green light in the additive context, I end up with white.

1.2

In additive synthesis, the primary colors are red, green, and blue

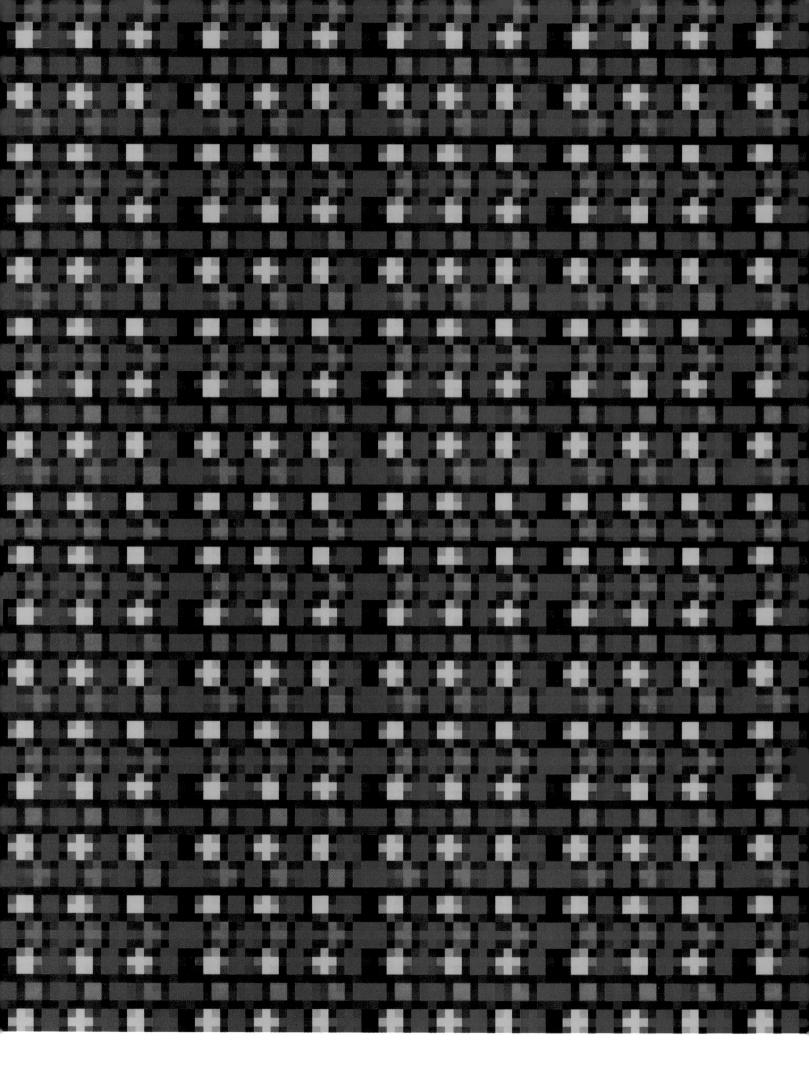

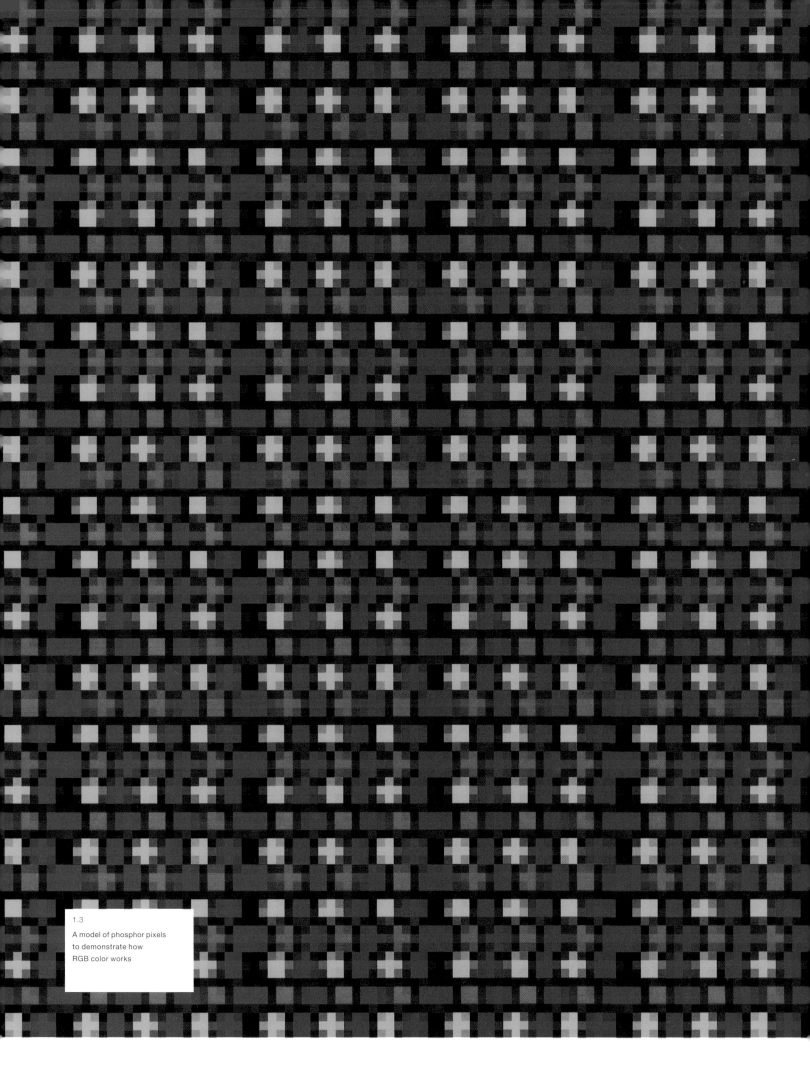

1.3
A model of phosphor pixels
to demonstrate how
RGB color works

Categories of Color in Detail

To gain an understanding of how colors create other colors, you'll examine color wheels and swatches in subtractive and additive synthesis.

As previously mentioned, the primary colors in subtractive synthesis are red, yellow, and blue. These are the colors from which all other organic colors become visible. Figure 1.4 shows the comparison of these primaries with the additive primary colors of red, green, and blue.

It's interesting to note that computer color, because of the variegations that exist in the way technology can generate the red, green, and blue, isn't as true to organic color. Remember, computer color comes from light and as such is a little more unstable. Typically, red will appear a little more orange than a true red, green tends to have more yellow in it, and blue contains more red, making it a bit more purple than true blue (Figure 1.5).

1.4
Comparing subtractive and additive primaries

1.5
Computer color
tends to be less than
true due to variegation
within hardware

In subtractive synthesis, add all the primary colors together to get black.
In additive synthesis, black is the absence of any light, 0 red, 0 green, 0 blue.
Similarly, black can be described as absence of light, and white as being light.

Secondary Colors

Once you've got the primaries as a base, secondary colors are achieved by mixing an equal amount of any two primary colors. Figure 1.6 shows the swatch of subtractive secondaries, which are orange, green, and purple respectively.

In the additive world, secondaries are achieved using the same ratio. The result of mixing equal amounts of additive primaries is shown in Figure 1.7. Red and green in equal amounts create yellow, red and blue in equal amounts create magenta, and green and blue in equal amounts create cyan.

1.6

Subtractive secondaries:
orange, green, purple

1.7

Additive secondaries:
yellow, magenta, cyan

Intermediate Colors

Tertiary Colors

When any two primaries are mixed together in a ratio of 2:1, the resulting color is referred to as an intermediate. Figure 1.8 shows intermediate colors in subtractive synthesis.

Tertiary colors are those colors that are created by mixing three primaries in different ratios. I mixed subtractive primaries using paint in 2:1:1 to come up with the following tertiary colors:

Burnt Orange:
two parts red, one part yellow, one part blue

Olive Green:
one part red, two parts yellow, one part blue

Reddish-Brown:
one part red, one part yellow, two parts blue

So, let's say if I were working with computer color, and I took two parts red, plus one part green, plus one part blue, I'd have a tertiary. In Figure 1.10, I created tertiary colors by using the following mixtures in 2:1:1 ratios:

Reddish-Brown:
two parts red, one part green, one part blue

Light Green:
one part red, two parts green, one part blue

Cornflower Blue:
one part red, one part green, two parts blue

1.8

Intermediate colors,
subtractive synthesis

1.9

Example of tertiary colors,
subtractive synthesis

two parts red
one part yellow
one part blue

one part red
two parts
yellow
one part blue

one part red
one part yellow
two parts blue

1.10

Example of tertiary colors,
additive synthesis

two parts red
one part green
one part blue

one part red
two parts green
one part blue

one part red
one part green
two parts blue

>   >

Tints are achieved by adding white (or adding light) to any given color, while shades are achieved by adding black (or removing light).

Tints and Shades

Tints occur by mixing any color, whether it be a primary, secondary, intermediate, or tertiary, with white (or light). Figure 1.11 shows examples of tints created from primaries.

Shades are achieved by adding black (or removing light) to darken a given color (Figure 1.12).

If you revisit history, you'll find a fascinating number and type of color prisms and wheels that mark different perspectives of color theory. Aristotle sought to determine the spatial relationship of color (Figure 1.13). In 1611, Aron Forsius suggested that there were five base colors: red, blue, green, yellow, and gray. According to Forsius, these colors formed the basis of all other colors (Figure 1.14). And a bit later in 1672, Sir Isaac Newton looked at sunlight through a prism and identified seven colors (Figure 1.15). Newton's notion that violet and red were related influenced the circular color wheel with which we are now so familiar. These prisms and wheels eventually culminated in the theories we work with in color today.

The standard twelve-segment color wheel describes the primary, secondary, and intermediate colors as they relate to one another. This is the color wheel with which you are likely to be most familiar. You've likely seen it in art books and in school—perhaps even in the playroom as a child (Figure 1.16). The subtractive wheel is what artists use as the fundamental resource for referring to when mixing paints and pigments, and it's the literal representation of the abstract ideas found in subtractive synthesis.

The additive color wheel (Figure 1.17) is based on the same concept of the standard, subtractive wheel. It portrays the primary, secondary, and intermediate colors found in additive synthesis. Of course, since all secondary and intermediate colors derive from mixtures of primary colors, the colors of the additive wheel are different from those of the subtractive using red, green, and blue as the primary colors rather than the subtractive primaries of red, yellow, and blue.

1.13

Aristotle saw
the spatial relationships
of colors

\>

If you revisit history, you'll find a fascinating number and type of color prisms and wheels that mark different perspectives of color theory.

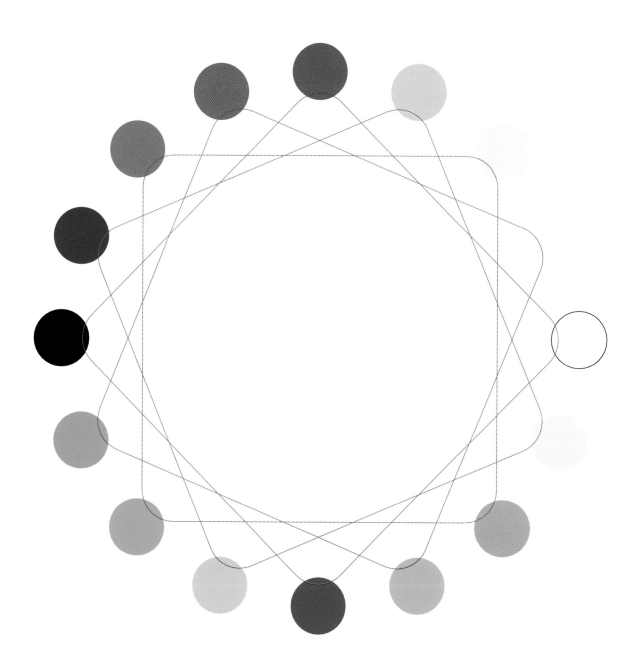

1.14

Forsius' colors used
a base of red, blue, green,
yellow, and gray to create
other colors in the wheel

1.15
Newton's color wheel

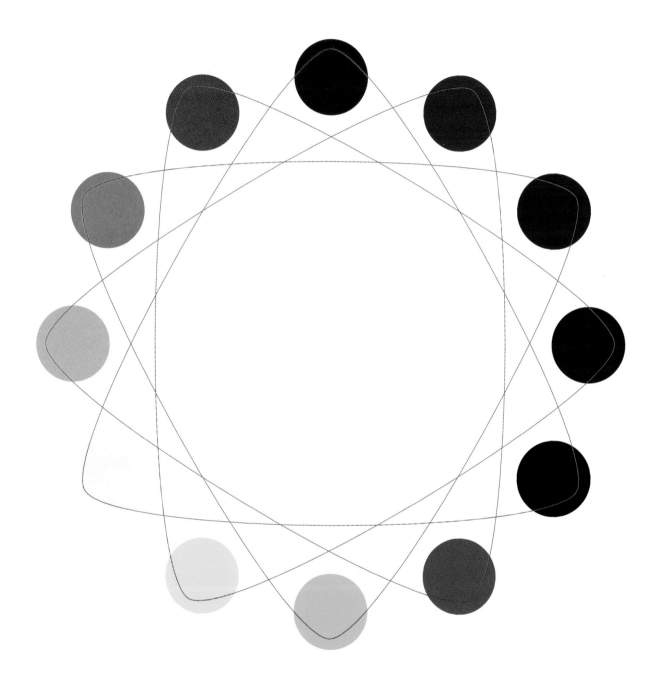

Newton's notion that violet and red were related influenced the circular color wheel with which we are now so familiar.

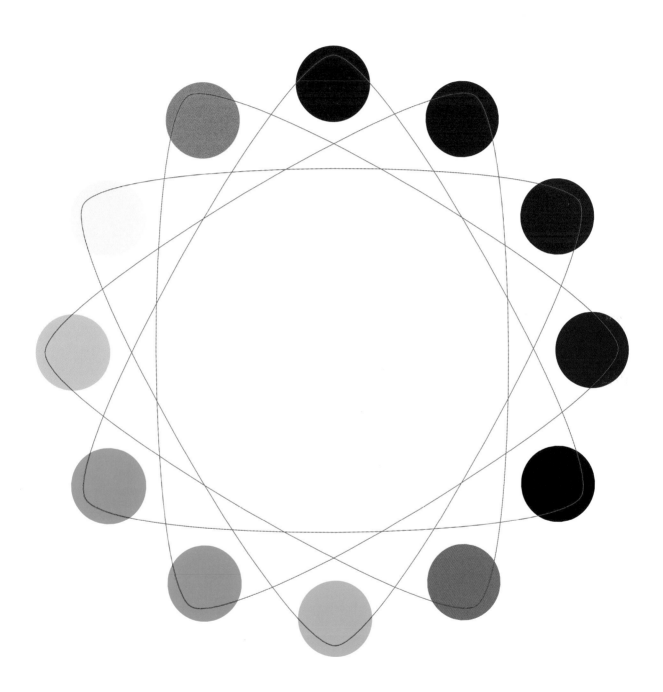

1.17
Familiar color wheel:
Additive synthesis

1.18

Hues within a spectrum

Properties of Color

Hue

Colors have different elements that make them unique. They have visual importance based on frequency, value, and intensity.

Individual colors are identified by hue (Figure 1.18), which is the wavelength frequency of a given color. As you know, red is different than green, and purple is different than brown. Hue is its unique identity of any color within the spectrum—that which differentiates it from another. Whether a color is primary, secondary, or intermediate, or is created from a subtractive or additive process isn't important with regard to hue. That an individual color exists as a unique entity defines hue.

Value

Earlier I discussed tints and shades, and described how adding white (or light) to a color (a hue) creates a tint. Similarly, adding black or removing light creates a shade. This is referred to as color value. Chocolate brown is darker than tan, and sky blue is lighter than navy. A color's value is defined by the amount of light or dark in that color.

Saturation (Intensity and Chroma)

Also referred to as intensity or chroma, you can think of saturation as being the brightness of a color. Peacock blue is very bright, whereas navy is rather dull. Similarly, those popular neon lime greens which bring to mind the 1960s are much more intense than a forest green (Figure 1.19).

To reduce intensity, other colors, black, white, or light are added or removed (Figure 1.20). A color is at its most intense and fully saturated when it is pure and unadulterated, where no black, white, or other color has been added to it.

1.19
Very bright,
highly saturated color

1.20
Low saturation

Color Relationships

Colors have relationships with one another. Just as people are both satisfied and challenged in their relationships, so color is satisfied and challenged by other colors around it.

Sometimes we are similar to the people in our lives, sometimes we are very different but complement one another with that difference. Sometimes we are very different from each other. Colors relate exactly the same way—they can be similar, complementary, contrasting. Harmonious relationships produce calm effects, relaxing the eye and conveying a sense of ease. Colors that catch your eye and irritate your mind are discordant.

The way in which colors relate to one another on the color wheel is a primary way in which we describe color relationships. There are four categories of this relationship: Complementary, Split-Complementary, Triad, and Analogous.

Complementary colors are those that appear directly across from one another on the color wheel (Figure 1.21). Complementary colors are considered to be high in contrast.

An interesting phenomenon of note to designers is the "after image." If you stared at a bright red box for a while, and then looked at a bright piece of paper, a blue box would appear. This after image is the color's complement! Interesting indeed.

Split-Complementary refers to the colors that appear to either side of a given color's complement. These colors also contrast, but not as stridently as a pure complementary color (Figure 1.22).

Triads are colors that are of equal distance from one another on the color wheel. Triad colors are often very harmonious and esthetically pleasing (Figure 1.23).

Analogous colors are those that appear next to one another on the color wheel. They are considered to be low in contrast, but are often easy to work with in combination because of their similarities to one another (Figure 1.24). Typically, these are referred to as monochromatic schemes.

1.21
Complementary Colors

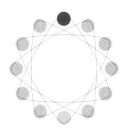 

1.22
Split-Complementary Colors

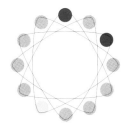 

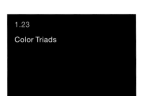

1.23
Color Triads

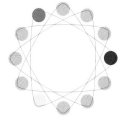 

1.24
Analogous Color

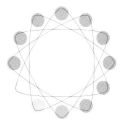 

Harmonious Color

Harmonious colors are those that work together with other colors to create a soothing, calm, and peaceful relationship. Typically, harmonious colors tend to be either close to one another on the color wheel, or equidistant (Figure 1.25).

Discordant Color

Colors that clash, cause nervousness, or appear particularly intense next to one another are considered to be discordant in nature. These colors are typically very high in contrast to one another (Figure 1.26).

1.25
Sample of harmonious colors

1.26
Yellow and black are discordant colors

Color can also be described in terms of temperature. Warm colors are those hues that are found in the yellow-to-red range (Figure 1.27). They project a sensation of heat. Cool colors are those colors in the range of green to blue. These colors convey brisk or even cold sensations (Figure 1.27). There are neutral colors, too. These colors are black, gray, white, and earth tones such as browns (Figure 1.28).

That colors have complex properties and relationships is not only interesting from a scientific perspective, but from an artistic one as well. How you as a designer will work to express color relies on your ability to understand what the properties of those colors are.

If you're working on a website for a spa, you're going to feel empowered by your knowledge of color relationships and temperature. To create your palette, you'll select colors that are harmonious and convey a sense of peace and relaxation. Similarly, if you're working for an athletic company to create a website that sells running shoes, you're going to want to look at more vibrant colors that express enthusiasm, and make people feel energetic and excited.

The power of color is such that if you as a designer make an error in color choice you can seriously compromise the efficacy of a website's message. If I were to create a website for a spa comprised of very vivid, energetic, and cold colors, I might intimidate potential clients who are looking for a week of total relaxation. Similarly, I wouldn't want to put my athletes to sleep by using very calm, harmonious colors in the opposite example.

1.27

Warm colors:
yellows, oranges, reds
Cool colors:
greens and blues

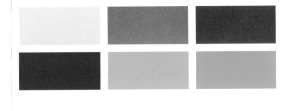

1.28

Neutral colors

WARM

COOL

If you're working on a website for a spa, you're going to be empowered by your knowledge of color relationships and temperature. To create your palette, you'll select colors that are harmonious and convey a sense of peace and relaxation.

CANYON RANCH.
HEALTH RESORT

TUCSON • ARIZONA

ABOUT THE LOCATION

TAKE OUR TOURS

ACTIVITIES

DINING

ACCOMMODATIONS

WHAT TO BRING

RATES

CALENDAR OF EVENTS

Call 800-742-9000 for more information.
© 1999, 2000, 2001
Canyon Ranch Management, L.L.C.,
and CR License, L.L.C.
All Rights Reserved

1.29
This website uses soft colors
to welcome the site visitor
and puts him or her
at ease

CANYON
RANCH.
HEALTH RESORT

WHAT IS CANYON RANCH?

CANYON RANCH PHILOSOPHY

The Canyon Ranch experience is all about healthy living. Canyon Ranch is a place to relax and learn how to deal effectively with the stress in your life while having a great time. And it can be so much more...

You'll find a variety of experiences to help you establish a healthy lifestyle and discover that it is possible to feel your best and enjoy life to the fullest. Your time at Canyon Ranch can be whatever you'd like it to be. It can be a structured set of classes, workshops and consultations where you can focus on your healthy stress levels, weight management, or a variety of other wellness concerns.

For some people, the Ranch is a modern day retreat for relaxation, pampering and to enjoy Ranch services in a tranquil setting. We have an experience to fit your lifestyle, travel plans and health goals.

Canyon Ranch can truly be a spa for all reasons.

BACK TO TOP

OUR HEALTHY LIFESTYLE

Since 1979, Canyon Ranch has set the standard for health spas all over the world. Today, you can experience Canyon Ranch through these venues:

- **Health Resorts**: It all began with Canyon Ranch's first health resort in the foothills of Tucson, Arizona's Sonoran desert. In 1989 Canyon Ranch in the Berkshires Health Resort was introduced amid the lush woodlands of Lenox, Massachusetts.
- **SpaClub**: Our 64,000-square-foot SpaClub - located in The Venetian Resort on the Las Vegas Strip - opened in 1999 as the industry's leading-edge fitness and health facility.

Every Canyon Ranch experience is an opportunity to explore your potential for the highest possible quality of life with:

- Spa services
- Fitness & outdoor sports
- Medical & behavioral services & consultations
- Nutrition consultations and workshops
- Spiritual pursuits
- Healthy gourmet cuisine

Learn to live your best while having a great time!

BACK TO TOP

BROWSE OUR BROCHURES

View and print any of these Canyon Ranch brochures. *You'll need Adobe Acrobat Reader.*

Health Resort in Tucson, Arizona

- Tucson Guide to Services
- Aquatic Center
- Golf Performance Center

Health Resort in Lenox, Massachusetts

- Lenox Guide to Services
- Special Health Packages & Sports Packages
- Group Getaways
- Meeting Retreats

BACK TO TOP

ALL ABOUT SPAS

Unlike most vacations, a spa experience can last long after you return home. Whether you are a first-time spa-goer or seasoned veteran, this information will help you make the most of a spa opportunity:

Spa-goer Tips
Glossary of Spa Terms

BACK TO TOP

CREATE YOUR OWN VISIT

Click here to search our Web site for a sample of the many opportunities that await you with a Canyon Ranch stay.

- CANYON RANCH PHILOSOPHY
- OUR HEALTHY LIFESTYLE
- BROWSE OUR BROCHURES
- ALL ABOUT SPAS
- CREATE YOUR OWN VISIT

OUR PURPOSE

At Canyon Ranch, our mission is to educate, motivate and inspire people to make a commitment to healthier living.

Similarly, if you're working for an athletic company to create a website that sells running shoes, you're going to want to look at more vibrant colors that express enthusiasm, and make people feel energetic and excited.

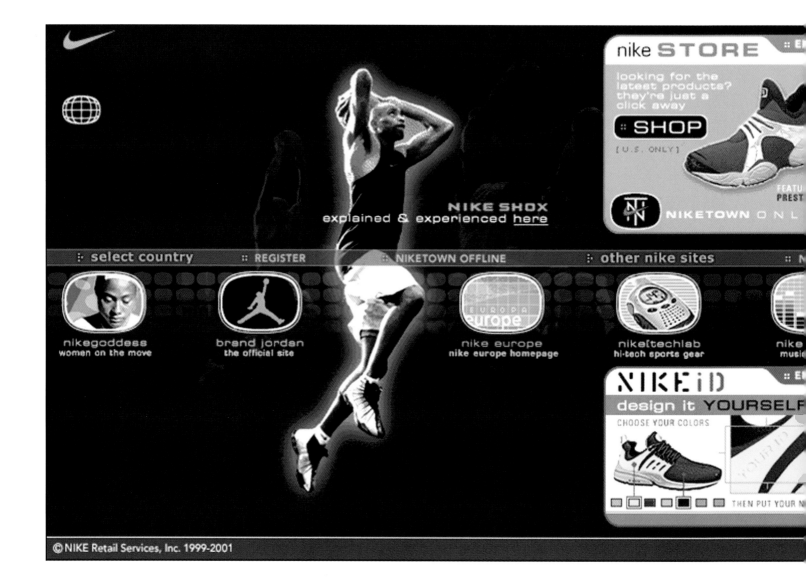

nike.com

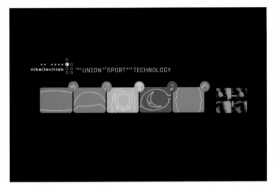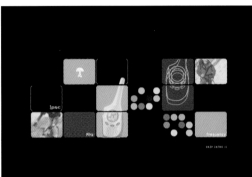

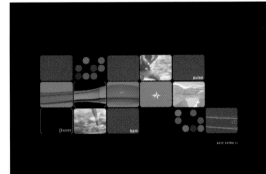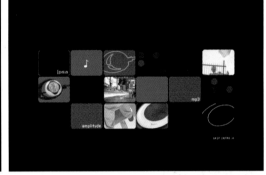

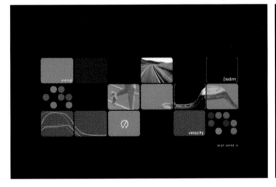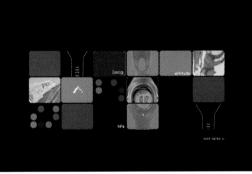

1.30

Nike's high contrast colors
serve to energize and invigorate
the visitor

The effects that appear in nature can be created by artists and designers to add visual intrigue and emotion to a design.

Color Effects

Luster

Beyond properties and relationships, there are special color effects. These effects occur mostly because of the way in which colors are combined together, or combined with light or dark.

Grab a piece of silk or satin from the closet. You'll find that these fabrics have a shine. Do you have a seashell somewhere in your home? Look at the inside of the shell, and you'll see a radiant, almost other-worldly light emanating from the colors.

The effects that appear in nature can be created by artists and designers to add visual intrigue and emotion to a design. Color effects include luster, iridescence, luminosity, transparency, and chroma.

The shiny effects that you see in silk or satin have to do with the fact that the visual perception of small areas of light combine with black contrast. While this is achieved naturally with a given fabric's relationship to light, artists can create it by relying on black contrast between the lustrous areas and the background (Figure 1.31).

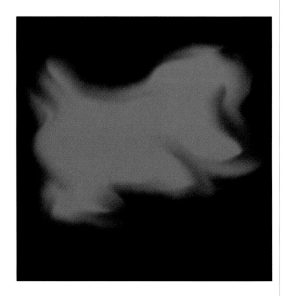

1.31
Luster is the visual perception of light and dark contrasts

Iridescence

Luminosity

As a child I loved to walk on the beach searching for seashells. I was undoubtedly drawn by their shapes, textures, and colors. The radiant visual effect found on the inside of a seashell is referred to as *iridescence* or *opalescence*. This effect occurs when gray and light are contrasted. A designer can achieve iridescence by using gray in the same areas of luster's black contrast (Figure 1.32).

The more delicate contrast is within a design, the more luminous it will appear. Luminosity relies on contrast just as luster and iridescence do. However, this contrast is extremely subtle, and the result is an almost unworldly effect (Figure 1.33).

1.32
Iridescence

1.33
Luminosity

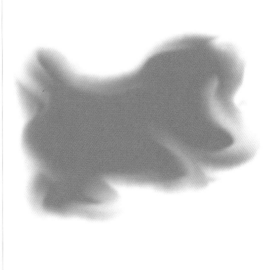

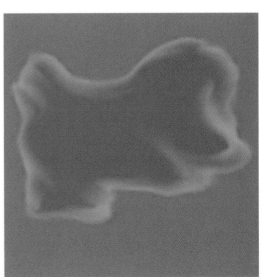

1.34

Transparency

The RGB color model is used by web designers and audiences, to control and view digital, on-screen colors.

Transparency

Color Models

Transparent colors are clear colors. The eye perceives transparency as being see-through (Figure 1.34).

In order to categorize color in some way that provides consistent communication of that color, the idea of Color Models came into being. Models of color are methods by which colors are grouped for specific purposes. RGB is a color model, and its primary use is to group and control digital, on-screen colors. Other color models that are important to become familiar with include HSV, CMYK, and Web safe.

The HSV/HSB color model is used in computer-based visual design software, such as Adobe Photoshop, for color correction and color manipulation.

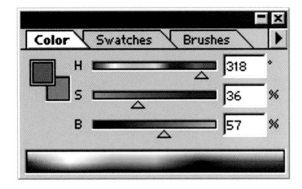

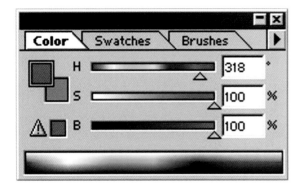

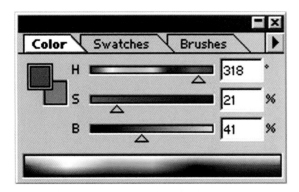

1.35

Working with the HSV/HSB color model

The top sample shows a color created with mixed percentages of hue, saturation, and brightness respectively

The middle example begins with the first hue, but describes a new, vivid hue at 100% saturation and brightness. When the saturation and brightness are dramatically reduced, the color becomes more muted

>

The CMYK model is used by printers and graphic designers for full color reproduction in printing, for instance, this book.

HSV/HSB

CMYK

The HSV color model is based on Hue, Saturation, and Value (or brightness). To attain a given color in the HSV model, percentages of hue, saturation, and brightness are mixed together.

Figure 1.35 shows three instances of the HSB palette in Photoshop 5.5. In each, I've mixed hue, saturation, and brightness in order to achieve a given color. The HSV/HSB color model is very common in computer-based visual design software. So, you'll probably encounter it a lot when working on your digital designs.

CMYK will be extremely familiar to those readers who are print designers. CMYK color, or *Cyan*, *Magenta*, *Yellow*, *Black*, is the color model used by printers. Whenever digital designers are preparing something for print, they typically work from this model, ensuring consistent color output.

Figure 1.36 shows an example of a CMYK color wheel. In this case, you'll see the three primary colors (cyan, magenta, yellow) and their secondary and intermediate colors within the wheel.

1.36

The CMYK color wheel

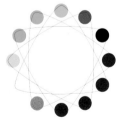

The Web-safe model limits colors to the 216 colors that have been deemed as "safe" for use on the Web.

Web Safe

The Web-safe color model is a relatively new model, only recently available in popular digital imaging software. The Web-safe model limits colors to the 216 colors that have been deemed as "safe" for use on the Web. In other words, these colors should appear consistent from one situation to the next, no matter the browser, platform, or hardware that an individual is using.

Web-safe color is RGB color, most frequently expressed in hexadecimal (base 12). Seeing that Chapter 2 examines Web color in great detail, I'll leave the history and methodology regarding Web-safe color to that chapter.

Figure 1.37 shows the Web safe sliders in Photoshop 5.5. You'll notice how the colors are interpreted in RGB and hex values, with the RGB values to the left of the sliders, and the hex values to the right.

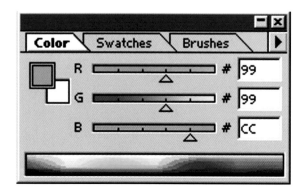

1.37

Web safe sliders
in Photoshop

From Here

With a good foundation of basic color theory behind you, it's time to look specifically to the Web, with its unique color challenges and opportunities. I'll begin with a look at color in a cross-browser, cross-platform context, and examine a case study where color and contrast created challenges based on many principles you've learned in this chapter.

Then, I'll dive more deeply into how browsers manage color, and how you can work with Web color to reach as consistent a state of color across browser types and platforms as possible. I'll also step you through the ways in which color is added to Web pages, showing you several different sophisticated and accurate methods of using Web mark-up to achieve color goals.

WORKING WITH
WEB COLOR

Chapter Two

\>

. . . gaining control over as many of the variations as possible is a goal that the meticulous designer strives to achieve, for their designs will then reach the broadest audience with the most consistent results.

Cross-Platform, Cross-Browser Color Design

No doubt you've heard the term "computer platform" bandied about. But just what is a computer platform? A computer platform consists of two components: an operating system and a microprocessor. By this definition, there's an implicit understanding that an integration of software and hardware must exist. The operating system and hardware work together to achieve desired computational results such as running a program, printing a document, or rendering colors and images on-screen.

As many readers are aware, there are multiple operating systems, and some share certain hardware specifications. For example, there are numerous versions of Windows, and all of them use an Intel or Intel-style microprocessor to run. Another popular operating system, MacOS, uses processors proprietary to Apple or Apple clone computers. Other operating systems, such as Unix or Linux, can run with a variety of microprocessors, depending upon the operating system's software type and version.

So how does this affect the Web designer? Well, software integrates with the platform to enable users to achieve a given result. A Web browser such as Microsoft Internet Explorer or Netscape Navigator works with their respective platform version to enable Web information to be displayed.

How this information is displayed in specific terms is dependent upon this and the addition of several other hardware and software components added to this integrated process. Video boards and monitors interact to provide the rendering of screen data. Operating systems contain technology that helps set contrast and correct gamma. The degree and variety of these components can be variegated, resulting in untold numbers of potential configurations and differences from one computer system to another.

The bane of the Web designer's existence is how to take these variations and create consistent screen results across platforms and browsers. This is no easy task. In fact, it's an impossible one! But gaining control over as many of the variations as possible is a goal that the meticulous designer strives to achieve, for their designs will then reach the broadest audience with the most consistent results.

A designer must first consider the multiple platform issue. From an audience perspective, it's helpful to know that many business and home users are using Windows operating systems. Design and print shops, artists, certain programmers and home users tend to prefer the MacOS. Then, there are networking and security specialists and open-source fanatics who use Unix, Linux and related systems.

With this in mind, consider then the different hardware within these systems. There are variations in processing speed, RAM, video cards and monitors. These complex configurations directly affect the number of colors a computer is able to display, as well as any gamma correction and contrast control.

The solution, after consideration of these issues, is that designers must test their work aggressively on major platform configurations with numerous versions and types of browsers on hand. For most designers, this boils down to Windows and Mac only, because they are the most popular computers for the home and business. However, in the Internet and computer industry, many people are using Unix and Linux, as well as other, more specialized platforms. Depending upon your audience, you may require a broader testing process.

If it sounds as though gaining control over color and image display is like herding cats, you're right. But the more you know about the variables, the better equipped you'll be to address them. So let's take a closer look at what they are, and then examine a real-world study in cross-platform, cross-browser design.

Gamma and the Computer Screen

The concept of gamma and contrast will be well-known to digital designers. But, for those who are unfamiliar with it, let me say very simply that gamma is a complex mathematical system influencing the display of information on a computer screen. In order to display color as accurately as possible, monitors are ideally calibrated and gamma corrected accordingly.

Of course, most home users—who are likely to be the majority of website visitors—never change the factory defaults to which their computers are configured. Different platforms offer different correction facilities, too. Macs and very high-end graphics machines such as those using the specialized SGI platform for digital production, video and film, have the best available

color correction. PCs using the Windows platform offer much less opportunities, particularly if the Windows OS is a dated one, prior to the 95 release. The better the video card and monitor with a contemporary Window OS, the better the built-in correction.

The main concern for Web designers concerned with color regarding gamma is that systems that offer limited gamma correction will display color and images that are quite dark in comparison to corrected environments. The perception of color—and as we will see in this chapter, shadow and light—is deeply affected by the way in which a given platform and hardware configuration renders the image on the screen.

2.1

Size contrast

low contrast

high contrast

2.3

High contrast is easy
to read, and the foreground
and background become
more distinct

2.4

The center colors are the same, but due to the matte color behind each swatch, the color on the right appears to be brighter than that on the left

Color Contrast

In art and design, contrast refers to any design element that is significantly different from another. So, if you have a large shape and a small one, the two shapes are contrasted in terms of their size (Figure 2.1).

Color contrast refers to the relationship of color differences. So, if a color is very different from another, it is said to have *high* contrast. Black and white have the most contrast than any colors because they are the most different from one another. On the color wheel, colors that appear across from one another (known as complementary color, see Chapter 1) are also considered to be contrasting colors. The closer a color is to another color, the less contrast those colors have.

Contrast is necessary for the human perception of color data to be apparent and discernable. People with normal vision and color perception require contrast to see image detail, read text, and respond on both the conscious and unconscious level to the colors with which they are interacting.

Without ample color contrast in design, the elements of that design become less distinct. Sometimes this is desirable. An artist may desire to create a low-contrast look. But for digital designers working on the Web, unless the site is particularly artistic or experimental, ample color contrast is necessary in order to visually convey a message.

When you combine the screen display problems that exist due to hardware and software differences in computer and Web technology, an understanding and awareness of color contrast becomes even more critical.

A good example of the importance of contrast is placing colored text on a colored background. If the colors used are too similar in value, the contrast will be low, and therefore difficult to read (Figure 2.2). In an example where you *want* that for subtle or mysterious effect, it can be successfully employed. But for the sake of readability, higher contrast is desirable (Figure 2.3).

A phenomenon referred to as *simultaneous contrast* (Figure 2.4) is the reality that, when one color is placed next to another, the colors' respective appearances change. This fascinating phenomenon can in turn cause frustration for designers trying to convey a specific mood or feeling. Or, in the case study you'll read about later in this chapter, the relationship of color to multiple colors in an image may significantly affect the outcome of the design.

So, when creating for the Web, color contrast must be chosen for the specific goals you wish to meet. If you want very readable material, employ a high contrast relationship between text and background. Looking to keep color meanings pure? Keep individual colors isolated in a similar field, or find colors whose influence upon the nearest color or image is minimal.

Capturing the Chaos

Gaining control over the variables involved in hardware
and software technology, much less the scientific
issues of gamma and contrast, is a challenge indeed.
It's especially difficult when working with colors
and images that are very detailed, such as those
containing gradients and plays on shadow and light.
While choosing the correct file formats for a given
image, or using color that is Websafe (discussed later
in this chapter) can assist a designer in gaining as
much control over the appearance of his or her digital
work, these methods cannot fully address the fact that
across browsers and across platforms, color will
appear darker or lighter. And, the darkness or
lightness of a given color, as I've already discussed in
Chapter 1, changes that color value, which in essence
really changes that color.

2.5
The processed illustration

2.6
The illustration against an olive
background

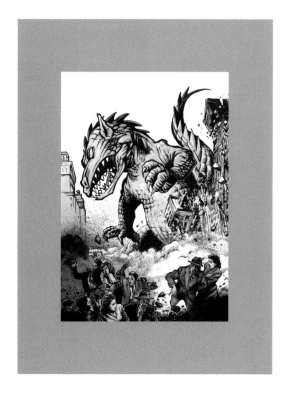

Case Study: Artist Joe Forkan's Website
http://www.joeforkan.com/

Working with artist Joe Forkan has helped me as a digital designer understand the cross-platform, cross-browser issues I've just described. Forkan approached me for assistance in getting his online portfolio together, and we decided we'd work together on the site. Forkan did the design and layout, and I assisted with choosing safe colors, producing his original graphics so they were Web-ready, and authoring the individual documents. We worked on his website in stages, with different parts of his current portfolio—Illustration, and Painting, each representing a different phase of the project.

First, we tackled his illustration work, which is often quite colorful. Forkan *envisioned* his work set against a muted olive green, pointing out that this color was becoming popular for backdrops when displaying contemporary artwork. The olive, which adds enough intrigue to the design without competing with the colors inherent to the illustrations, worked well with most of the illustrations regardless of their contrast concerns.

This is clearly illustrated in "Monster," a lively and stylized print illustration Forkan did for the cover of the Tucson Weekly in 1998 (Figure 2.5). When processed for the Web, the bright colors and detailed strokes were easily maintained and looked good against the olive green of the site background (Figure 2.6). I tested the results on the two primary platforms felt to make up his potential audience: Windows and Mac. I found some differences, but not enough to cause problems. The inherent qualities of bright color and detail express equally well across platforms and browsers.

Another cover illustration, "Napoleon," this time for the Los Angeles New Times, depicts Napoleon standing on the bodies of young children (Figure 2.7). The related story, "The Emperor of Ignorance," covered a Californian school official's policies regarding bilingual education for children. Forkan's irony is emphasized by the paradoxical light gradient surrounding the main figure against the darker, tragic bodies of the children beneath. Maintaining this gradient and ensuring the detail of the bodies illustrates an example where the maintenance of light and dark require some thought in production. In production, I was able to address the concern quite well using the proper file format, with no additional work to the image to get acceptable results across platforms.

But the problem becomes slightly compounded when the artist's work gets darker in its inherent design and the media in which it's created. In "Uncle Sam," Forkan's cartoon, illustration, and painting skills combine to convey deep commentary regarding U.S. involvement in the South American drug trade (Figure 2.8). In this instance, the dark hues in the work appear significantly darker on a PC versus a Macintosh machine, but still within acceptable means.

Even black-and-white illustrated pieces, such as "Oswald" and "Saddam" rendered well because the inherent contrast of the illustrations is intact, and managed to convey across platforms (Figures 2.9 and 2.10).

Given the overall cross-browser, cross-platform success with Forkan's illustration work, no problems were expected in the next phase, the painting phase.

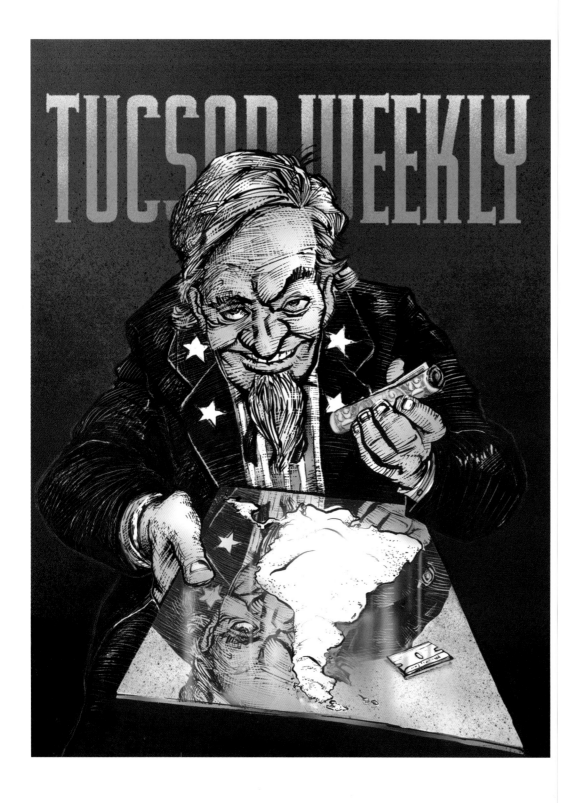

Contrast within
this illustration is intact,
so it conveys well
on the Web

2.10

Another example
where contrast is inherent
to the image

Forkan, who paints primarily in oil on panel, tends to choose dark tints and uses a range of stroke types in his painting. How could I render these paintings, which in the real world are layered, precise works, on-screen with the best possible results? It proved difficult indeed.

When I moved on to the painting and monotype section of Forkan's portfolio, I processed some tests using a PC for Forkan to look at. In Windows, the tests looked fine. But when he looked at the tests on the Mac, it became quickly evident that the quality of the screen renderings were simply unacceptable.

Another challenge was how to convey the emotional impact of paintings across a computer screen. The organic nature of paint, the unique quality of the strokes, and the size of many of his paintings, such as "Dummy"—a large painting (48 x 60 inches) which commands any space it's in—gave me pause (Figure 2.11). How was I to preserve the painting's imposing reality? Beyond that, the movement and colors in the sky and water contrasted with the disconcerting stillness of the figures required the maintenance of as much color integrity as we could muster. I processed the image and was fairly pleased with the results when saved to a high JPEG format. But, when the image was placed on the olive background, Forkan was unhappy with the results (Figure 2.12). The olive created a brighter, more active atmosphere, detracting from the strength and colors native to the painting itself.

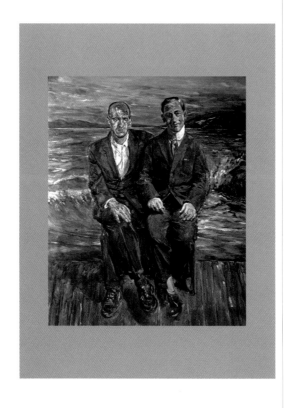

2.11

The processed image preserved many elements of the painting: strokes, movement, impact

2.12

Placing this painting on the olive matte caused the potency of the image to conflict with the brightness of the background

This problem became increasingly obvious as the production of work on other paintings continued. Take "Substance for the Shadow" for example (Figure 2.13). This arresting work mixes a breathtaking vulnerability when perceived as a deeply tender moment for lovers with dark questions (is the female figure ill? Dead?). The deep greens and reds of the painting became amplified when the bright olive green background began to compete for attention, affecting the impact and emotion of the painting's subject (Figure 2.14).

The problem in this case—at least one of them—is the issue regarding simultaneous contrast. The color surrounding the artwork was affecting the colors *within* the artwork. Another problem had to do with the dark and light relationships described during the production of the illustrations. While "Dummy" and "Substance for the Shadow" have more contrast within the paintings themselves, much of Forkan's painting is about imagery emerging from obscurity, from darkness—from memory, perhaps, or other dimensions of thought.

2.13
This painting contains a lot of green strokes

2.14
When placed against the olive background, a competition for attention between the painting and matte space occurred

This is clearly seen in "Bastard." The painting's very existence is meant to evoke mystery, questions (Figure 2.15). There's nothing clear here, and the artist has created only portions of figures. What is their relationship? Their gender? Their age? We are compelled to move closer to the work and explore what is emerging from the void beyond. The painting relies on very subtle contrasts to achieve its impact.

How would this convey on-screen if the environment isn't neutral enough to let what is emerging from the painting to emerge completely, without conflicting with any other color elements? The olive green background of the site distracts us because it is too bright compared to the subtle colors and contrast within the painting (Figure 2.16). This inhibits the emotional process of moving into the emotional dimensions of the work.

2.15

This painting relies on low contrast to convey its meaning

2.16

Against the olive, the low contrast of the painting is increased, with the end result that it actually loses visual impact

We set aside the paintings for a bit and moved on to work with Forkan's monotypes. A monotype is a print-making technique in which the artist draws the image with paint or ink on a smooth surface such as zinc or Plexiglas. Then the plate is run through a printing press, transferring the image to paper. Forkan uses this technique a great deal. Sometimes, he'll add scratches and color to the monotype after it's printed, other times he'll create second, or "ghost" prints of the monotype for added effect.

The first monotype we struggled with was "Portrait of Rainer." Rainer Ptácek, an internationally acclaimed guitar and dobro player, lost his life to brain cancer at the age of 46. An East-German born Czech raised in Chicago, Rainer's music influenced many musicians, including Robert Plant and Howe Gelb. But Rainer chose to live a modest life down here in Tucson's desert, despite the worldwide, enthusiastic audience that he had acquired over the years. As such, his relationships with the Tucson creative scene—its musicians, writers, and artists—are ones that went very deep and have, with his death, been elevated to deserving legendary status.

Forkan's monotype portrait of Rainer is a legacy work. It stands as a gift of the soul, given from one artist to another artist held dear, and in its digital form, from artist to the world via the Web. It's impossible to take this piece lightly. We had to find the solution to the problems we were finding with color, light, and contrast in Forkan's work and come to some acceptable medium (Figure 2.17).

First, we thought to sharpen the image in the hope of making the lines more readily visible to site visitors, no matter their platform or browser. The sharp filter did bring out the lines, but made them too harsh, ruining the softer details of this visionary's face (Figure 2.18). That wasn't the solution, certainly.

Back to the original. Now, we tried to brighten the original. It worked a little better, giving us good results on the Mac, but still darker results on Windows. So then we tried to fiddle with the contrast, and here we found at least part of the solution (Figure 2.19).

In this version, we used Photoshop to increase the contrast of the original by 25. This increase gave us acceptable results across platforms (Figure 2.20). Perfect? No. But as I mentioned at the start of this chapter, these issues are the Web designer's bane of existence. There was nothing we could do to achieve perfection, but we could get close. And we felt that this was as close as it was going to get.

2.17

The original monotype image was too dark on the PC, even though it looked acceptable on a Mac

2.18

Sharpening the image made the lines of the work too harsh

2.19

Brightening the image worked better, but still proved too dark

2.20

Adding contrast proved to render the most acceptable results

Simultaneous Conflict

When we added the resulting image into the site template and viewed it on the Mac and PC, we were frustrated to find that as with the other paintings still in production, the olive green was arguing with the subtle aspects of the monotype.

At this point, we realized we had to resolve the background color conflict by changing the color. As we examined this concern, we were aware of several things. First, the background color would have to be neutral enough to blend with the paintings and monotypes, but not compete or diminish them in any way. And, the color would also have to integrate well with the colors used for the illustration area of the site, where the olive was working well. We had to find a color that would also integrate the other colors in the main site into the painting section of the site as seamlessly as possible, maintaining the integrity of the design as a whole.

If we had chosen white, the contrast between bright white and the subtle wonders within a monotype such as "Cruel Memory" would be compromised (Figure 2.21). Black was better, for some, but too dark for very dark monotypes, such as "Tide" (Figure 2.22).

So we settled on a medium gray, and finally, the solution was at hand. We worked the contrast process for other monotypes, including "Cruel Memory" and "Tide." Each of these pieces has different contrast qualities from the Rainer monotype (Figure 2.20). "Cruel Memory" has much more defined sections of light and dark, and "Tide" is extremely low contrast, with very little light to discern the figure from the imposing darkness. We boosted the contrast in each case, and it worked well when placed upon the medium gray background (Figure 2.23).

In order to complete the painting section of the site, we processed all the paintings with the +25 contrast and used the medium gray background for the site. The results are very acceptable across platforms, combining the best possible retention of the art and its emotion born of color, light, and shadow with the limitations of the Web.

2.21

The white background is too harsh for the subtlety of this work

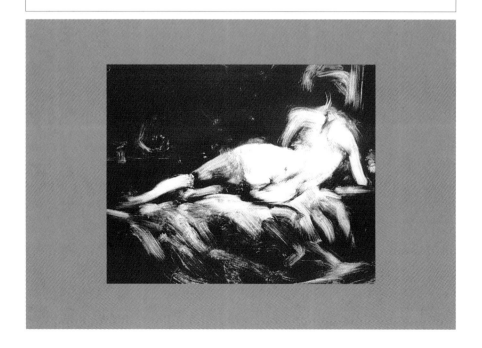

2.23

A medium gray enhanced the experience of this monotype

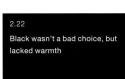

2.22
Black wasn't a bad choice, but lacked warmth

2.24
The very low contrast of this image doesn't compete in any way with the background

Computer Platforms and Color

As if issues of consistent color and contrast between images and the screen weren't challenging enough, their exists the issue of interoperable color. The problems with Web color being consistent from screen to screen evolve both from the platform issues described earlier in this chapter as well as browsers themselves.

From a technical perspective, computers can display a range of colors on-screen, depending upon the relationship that computer has with the platform it's on, and the type of video memory that's available. This, combined with the layout of a computer screen—which is essentially a grid made up of many small boxes (Figure 2.25). These boxes are what we refer to as pixels.

Color is distributed on this grid, combining the additive principles (see Chapter 1) with a mathematical approach that allows each pixel to be allotted an amount of that video memory. The amount of memory in question is referred to as a bit, and depending upon the amount of bits and the amount of pixels available, the type and quality of color is affected.

Lowest on the totem pole when it comes to color management on-screen is one bit being allocated to a pixel. This will result in only two colors being supported. One-bit systems were very common once upon a time (Figure 2.26), but of course now are almost unheard of—especially for home computer users and most certainly for high-end designers.

The next level of color is known as 8 bit color. When 8 bits of color are allotted to a single pixel, the resulting number of possible colors is 256. This is an important number when it comes to how Web color works, as you'll soon see. Suffice to say for the moment that 256 color systems are in popular use, although again, the proliferation of higher-end systems for home users as well as the specialty systems used by designers make 8 bit color systems less important as time goes on—at least when it comes to how Web color is produced

(Figure 2.27). 16 bit color appears in those systems which allot 16 bits of video RAM to a pixel. The resulting number of colors is in the thousands, which naturally offers a radical increase in the quality of the color displayed on-screen. But interestingly enough, the 16 bit color model is very different from both the 256 colors below it, and the millions of colors above it. This is due to the fact that 16 bit color, also referred to as *High Color*, is based on a system of percentages. As a result, the colors in high color may or may not have cross-over colors from either the lower or higher ends of color management.

Finally, *True Color* monitors are those capable of managing 24 bits of RAM per pixel. This in turn creates millions—specifically 16,777,216—resulting colors. It's important to point out that this palette is more mathematically in step with the methods by which the 256 color systems work. As a result, all 256 colors in the 8 bit system are also found in the 24 bit system.

2.26

A one-bit monochromatic system

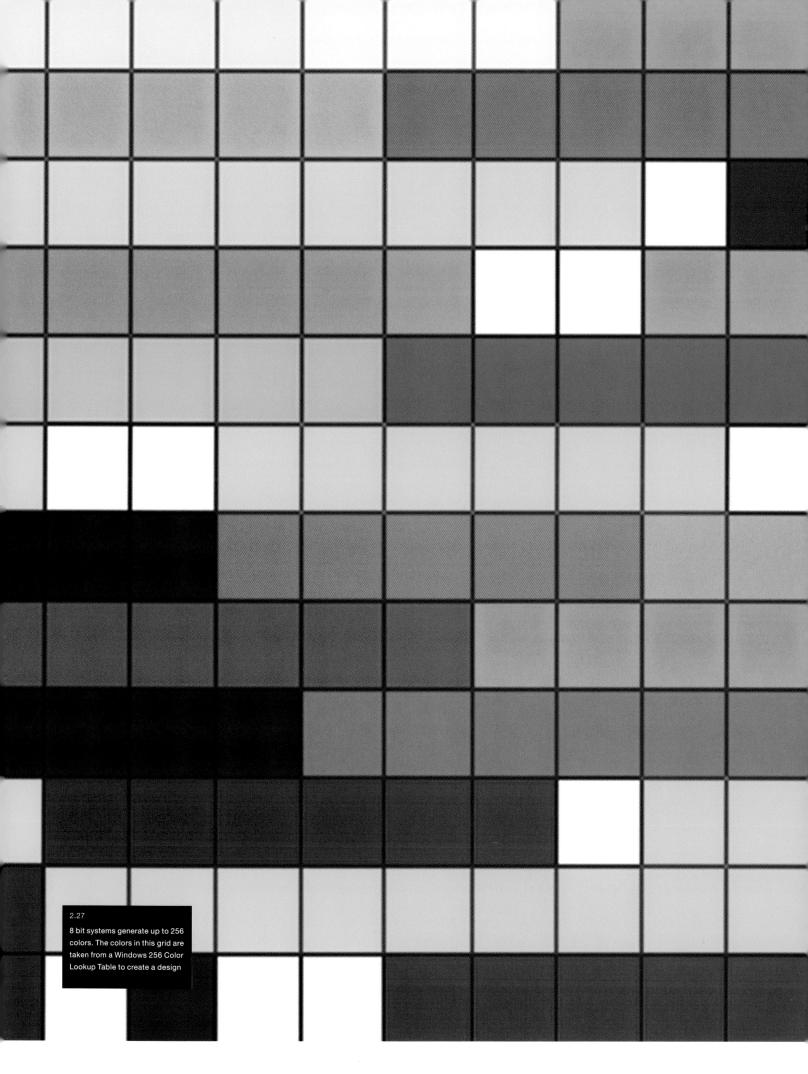

2.27
8 bit systems generate up to 256 colors. The colors in this grid are taken from a Windows 256 Color Lookup Table to create a design

Color For Browsers

If you've been working in Web design for a while, you have already heard of the Web-safe (also known as *Browser-safe*) palette. This palette consists of 216 colors that are expected to remain stable across two platforms: Mac and Windows.

But if color systems can support at least 256 colors and at best millions of colors, why is the Web-safe palette so limited? It's an historical issue, and one that I'll describe here in order to make the case that the use of this palette is important but not always necessary.

While this chapter is about working with Web color, you'll notice I've spent a lot of time on cross-browser, cross-platform concerns. This is because in reality, you'll never get consistent color across browsers and platforms. There are simply too many variables. However, it's extremely important to reach for the most consistency, and this is exactly how Web-safe color evolved.

When the Web became a visual space in 1993, most Macintosh and Windows computers were 8 bit, 256 color. Each platform reserves about 20 colors for use by the system, and there are differences between the color tables found in those platforms (Figures 2.28 and 2.29). All told, in an 8 bit system, the differences total 40 varying colors. If a designer uses an unsupported color, the potential of dithering is high in 8 bit systems—the computer will pick the closest possible color. Other problems include grabbing a different color completely, so a light pastel pink might suddenly become neon pink on another system. This is, for obvious reasons, very problematic.

To reduce the cross-browser, cross-platform problems, Netscape eliminated the 40 inconsistent colors and created a browser-specific palette of 216 colors. Ideally, using these colors reduces dithering and other color rendering problems across platforms. Hence, the Web-safe palette was born (Figure 2.30).

But now that computers support 16 and 24 bit color, the browser-safe issue becomes less of a concern in certain instances. However, many designers choose to stick to the browser-safe palette because there are still many computers—particularly those in schools, foreign countries, and other arenas—that are limited to 256 colors. By sticking to the Web-safe palette, designs achieve greater consistency.

But all is not perfect in the so-called Web-safe world. Why not? Well, consider the earlier discussion that describes how 16 bit systems and 24 bit systems are different. So your colors might appear slightly different on a 16 bit system and a 24 bit system, even if you're using the Web-safe palette. What's more, several concerned parties began to look closely at the emerging concerns surrounding Web-safe colors and found some very disconcerting evidence that what we *think* is Web-safe is really not safe at all.

In January, 1999, Bob Stein of VisiBone performed some tests across monitors. His results suggest that there are only 125 truly safe colors from which to choose (Figure 2.31). Stein does point out that some of this problem might be hardware and some of it might be related to eyesight.

A later test, performed by David Lehn and Hadley Stern for WebMonkey in September of 2000 looked at colors across system types, browser types, and computer types and ended up with a staggering number of *only 22 colors* that could be considered more or less truly Web-safe (Figure 2.32). And, looking at these colors, you'll see they're very limited and not the most attractive!

2.28

256 Color Lookup Table,
Macintosh

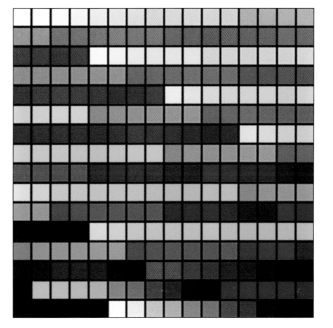

2.29

256 Color Lookup Table,
Windows

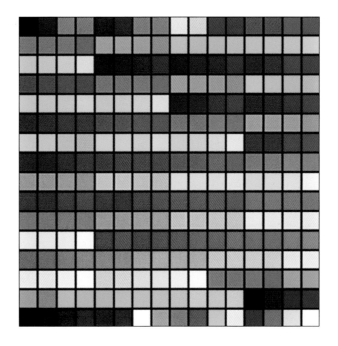

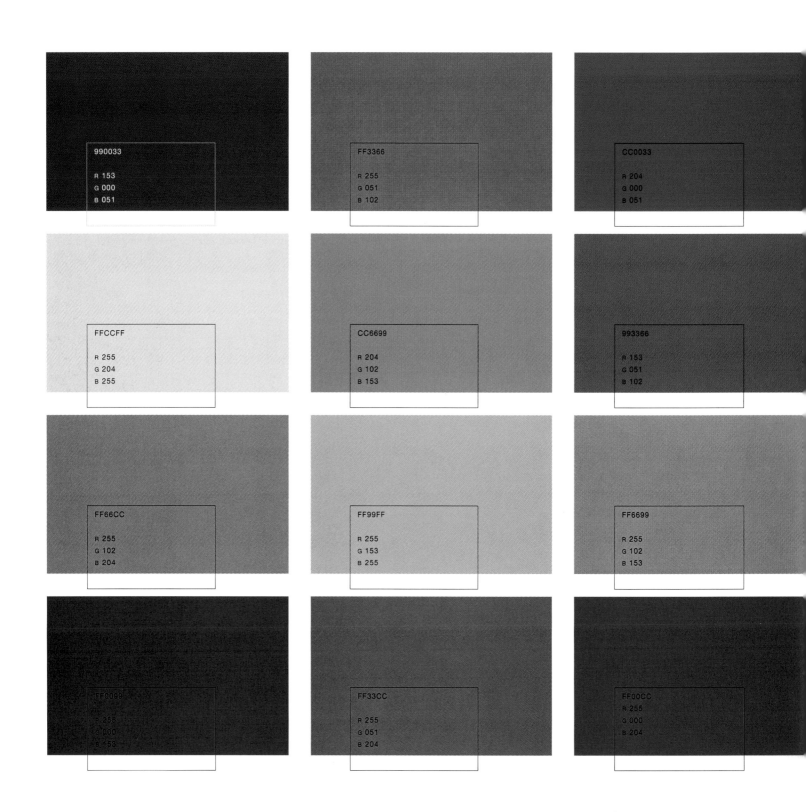

990033

R 153
G 000
B 051

FF3366

R 255
G 051
B 102

CC0033

R 204
G 000
B 051

FFCCFF

R 255
G 204
B 255

CC6699

R 204
G 102
B 153

993366

R 153
G 051
B 102

FF66CC

R 255
G 102
B 204

FF99FF

R 255
G 153
B 255

FF6699

R 255
G 102
B 153

FF0099

R 255
G 000
B 153

FF33CC

R 255
G 051
B 204

FF00CC

R 255
G 000
B 204

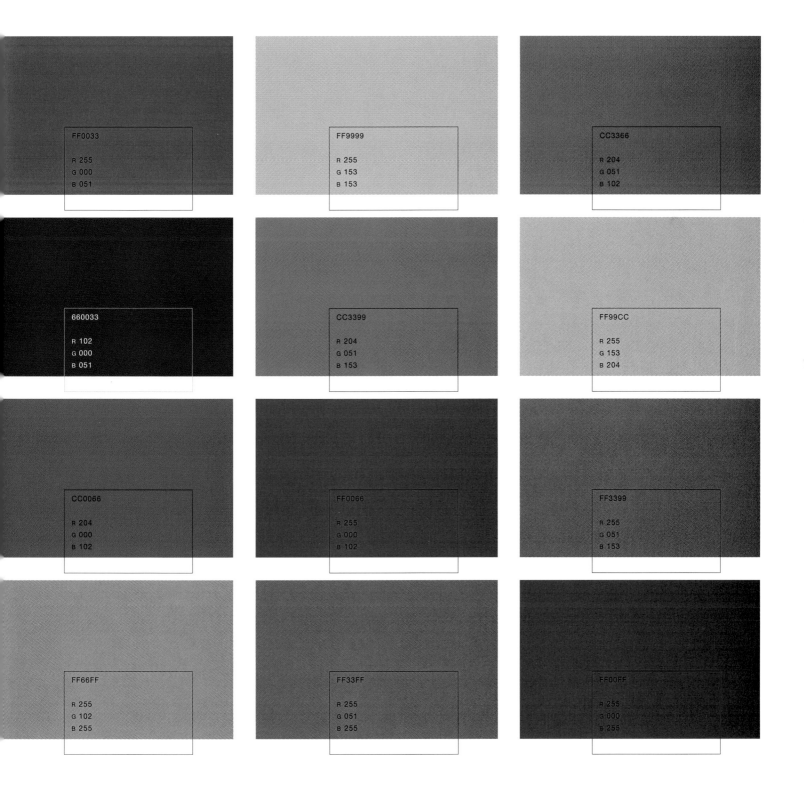

FF0033

R 255
G 000
B 051

FF9999

R 255
G 153
B 153

CC3366

R 204
G 051
B 102

660033

R 102
G 000
B 051

CC3399

R 204
G 051
B 153

FF99CC

R 255
G 153
B 204

CC0066

R 204
G 000
B 102

FF0066

R 255
G 000
B 102

FF3399

R 255
G 051
B 153

FF66FF

R 255
G 102
B 255

FF33FF

R 255
G 051
B 255

FF00FF

R 255
G 000
B 255

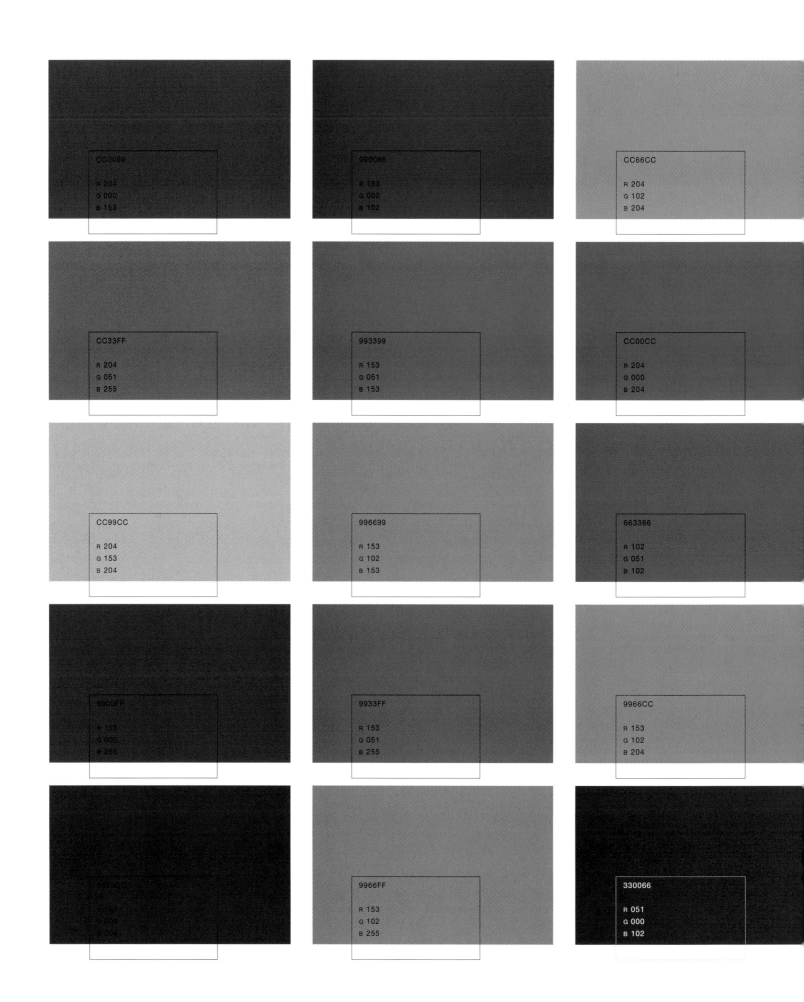

CC0099

R 204
G 000
B 153

990066

R 153
G 000
B 102

CC66CC

R 204
G 102
B 204

CC33FF

R 204
G 051
B 255

993399

R 153
G 051
B 153

CC00CC

R 204
G 000
B 204

CC99CC

R 204
G 153
B 204

996699

R 153
G 102
B 153

663366

R 102
G 051
B 102

9900FF

R 153
G 000
B 255

9933FF

R 153
G 051
B 255

9966CC

R 153
G 102
B 204

9900CC

R 153
G 000
B 204

9966FF

R 153
G 102
B 255

330066

R 051
G 000
B 102

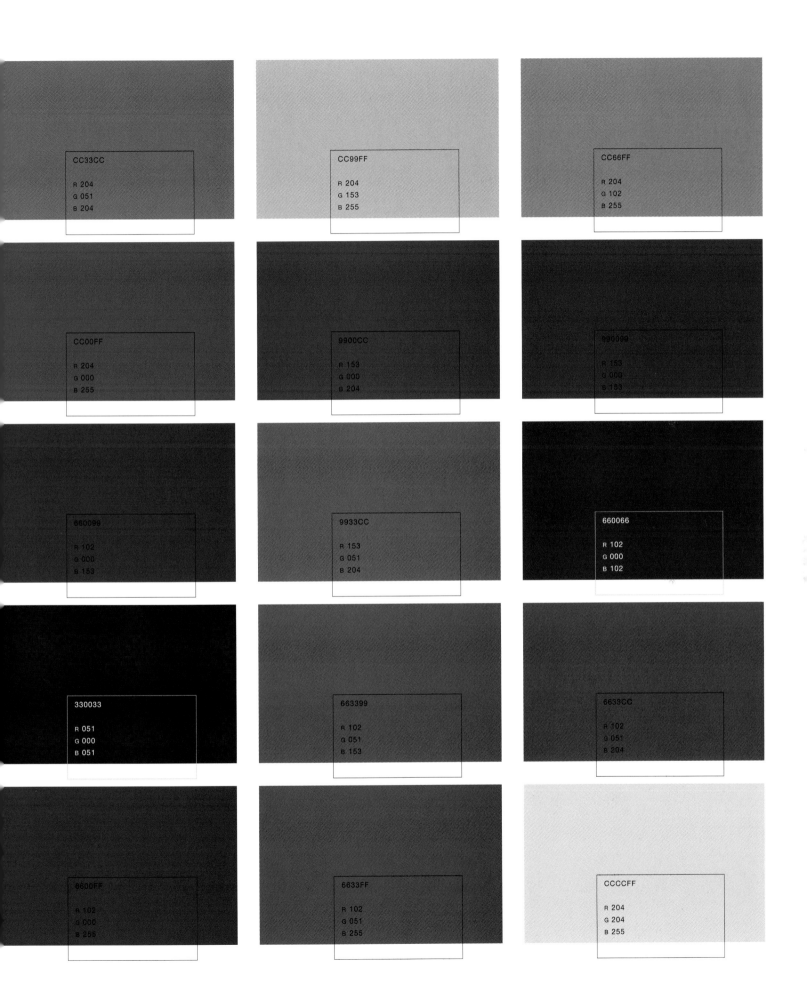

CC33CC

R 204
G 051
B 204

CC99FF

R 204
G 153
B 255

CC66FF

R 204
G 102
B 255

CC00FF

R 204
G 000
B 255

9900CC

R 153
G 000
B 204

990099

R 153
G 000
B 153

660099

R 102
G 000
B 153

9933CC

R 153
G 051
B 204

660066

R 102
G 000
B 102

330033

R 051
G 000
B 051

663399

R 102
G 051
B 153

6633CC

R 102
G 051
B 204

6600FF

R 102
G 000
B 255

6633FF

R 102
G 051
B 255

CCCCFF

R 204
G 204
B 255

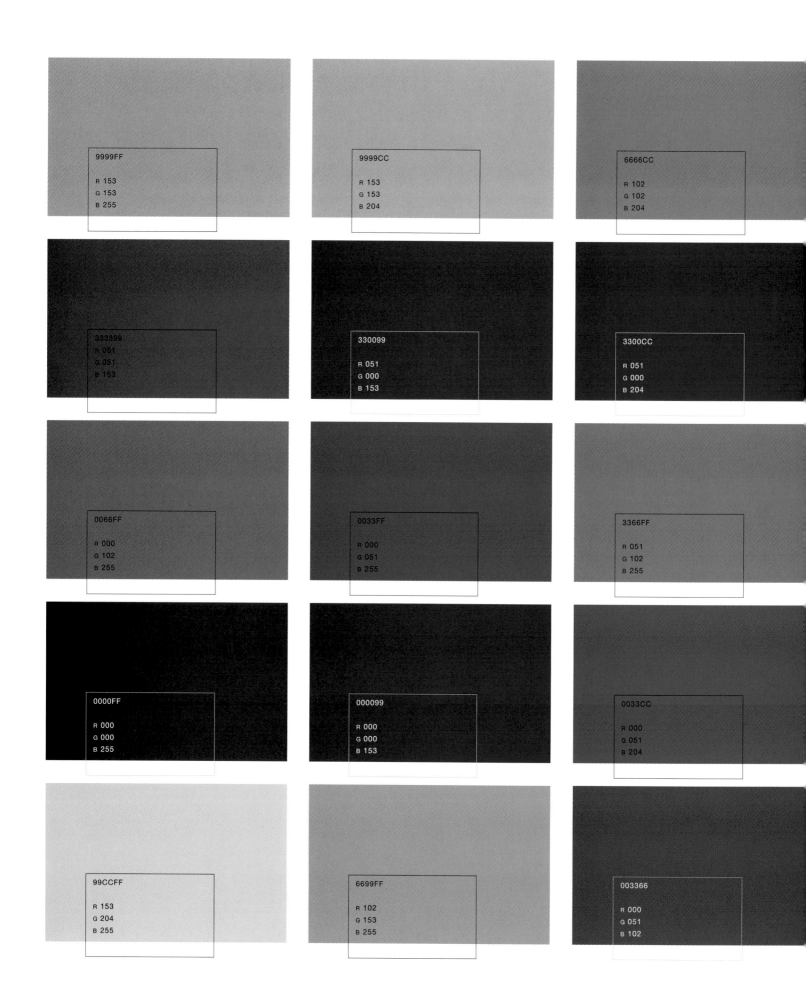

9999FF

R 153
G 153
B 255

9999CC

R 153
G 153
B 204

6666CC

R 102
G 102
B 204

333399
R 051
G 051
B 153

330099

R 051
G 000
B 153

3300CC

R 051
G 000
B 204

0066FF

R 000
G 102
B 255

0033FF

R 000
G 051
B 255

3366FF

R 051
G 102
B 255

0000FF

R 000
G 000
B 255

000099

R 000
G 000
B 153

0033CC

R 000
G 051
B 204

99CCFF

R 153
G 204
B 255

6699FF

R 102
G 153
B 255

003366

R 000
G 051
B 102

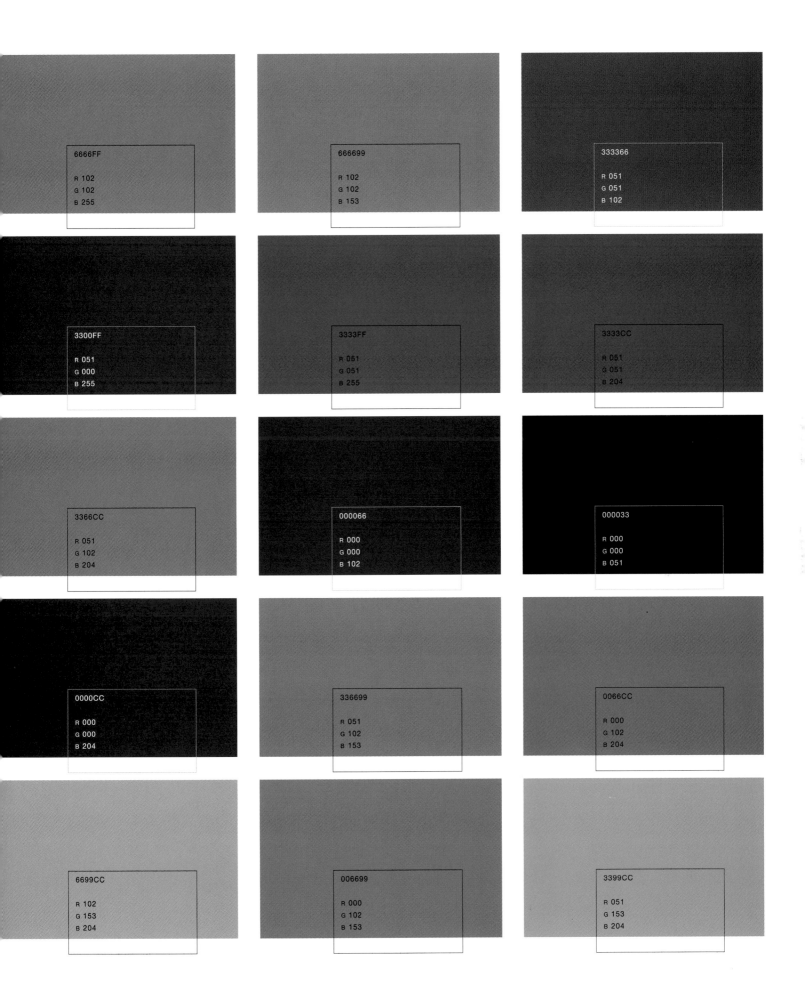

6666FF

R 102
G 102
B 255

666699

R 102
G 102
B 153

333366

R 051
G 051
B 102

3300FF

R 051
G 000
B 255

3333FF

R 051
G 051
B 255

3333CC

R 051
G 051
B 204

3366CC

R 051
G 102
B 204

000066

R 000
G 000
B 102

000033

R 000
G 000
B 051

0000CC

R 000
G 000
B 204

336699

R 051
G 102
B 153

0066CC

R 000
G 102
B 204

6699CC

R 102
G 153
B 204

006699

R 000
G 102
B 153

3399CC

R 051
G 153
B 204

0099CC

R 000
G 153
B 204

66CCFF

R 102
G 204
B 255

3399FF

R 051
G 153
B 255

00CCFF

R 000
G 204
B 255

99FFFF

R 153
G 255
B 255

66FFFF

R 102
G 255
B 255

009999

R 000
G 153
B 153

669999

R 102
G 153
B 153

99CCCC

R 153
G 204
B 204

339999

R 051
G 153
B 153

336666

R 051
G 102
B 102

006666

R 000
G 102
B 102

33CC99

R 051
G 204
B 153

00CC99

R 000
G 204
B 153

66FFCC

R 102
G 255
B 204

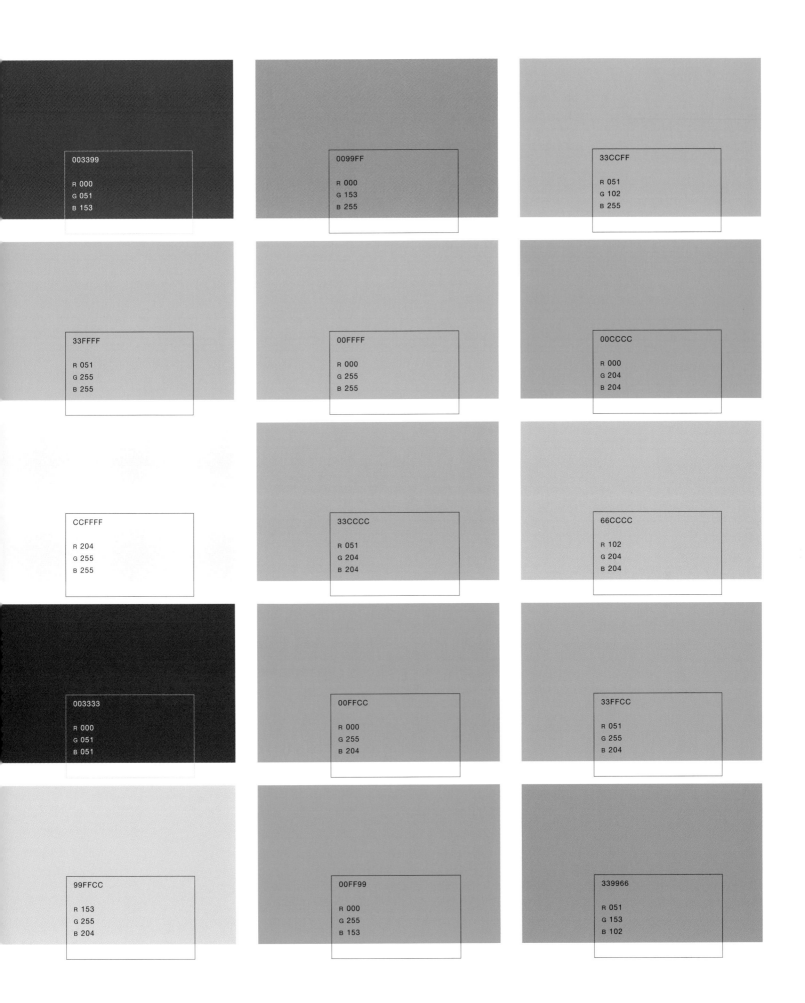

003399
R 000
G 051
B 153

0099FF
R 000
G 153
B 255

33CCFF
R 051
G 102
B 255

33FFFF
R 051
G 255
B 255

00FFFF
R 000
G 255
B 255

00CCCC
R 000
G 204
B 204

CCFFFF
R 204
G 255
B 255

33CCCC
R 051
G 204
B 204

66CCCC
R 102
G 204
B 204

003333
R 000
G 051
B 051

00FFCC
R 000
G 255
B 204

33FFCC
R 051
G 255
B 204

99FFCC
R 153
G 255
B 204

00FF99
R 000
G 255
B 153

339966
R 051
G 153
B 102

006633

R 000
G 102
B 051

336633

R 051
G 102
B 051

669966

R 102
G 153
B 102

339933

R 051
G 153
B 051

99CC99

R 153
G 204
B 153

66FF99

R 102
G 255
B 153

66CC99

R 102
G 204
B 153

009966

R 000
G 153
B 102

009933

R 00
G 153
B 051

CCFF99

R 204
G 255
B 153

99FF66

R 153
G 255
B 102

99FF33

R 153
G 255
B 051

33CC33

R 051
G 204
B 051

66FF33

R 102
G 255
B 051

00FF00

R 000
G 255
B 000

66CC66

R 102
G 204
B 102

99FF99

R 153
G 255
B 153

66FF66

R 102
G 255
B 102

33FF99

R 051
G 255
B 153

33CC66

R 051
G 204
B 102

00CC66

R 000
G 204
B 102

33FF66

R 051
G 255
B 102

00FF66

R 000
G 255
B 102

CCFFCC

R 204
G 255
B 204

00FF33

R 000
G 255
B 051

33FF33

R 051
G 255
B 051

00CC33

R 000
G 204
B 051

66CC33

R 102
G 204
B 051

006600

R 000
G 102
B 000

003300

R 000
G 051
B 000

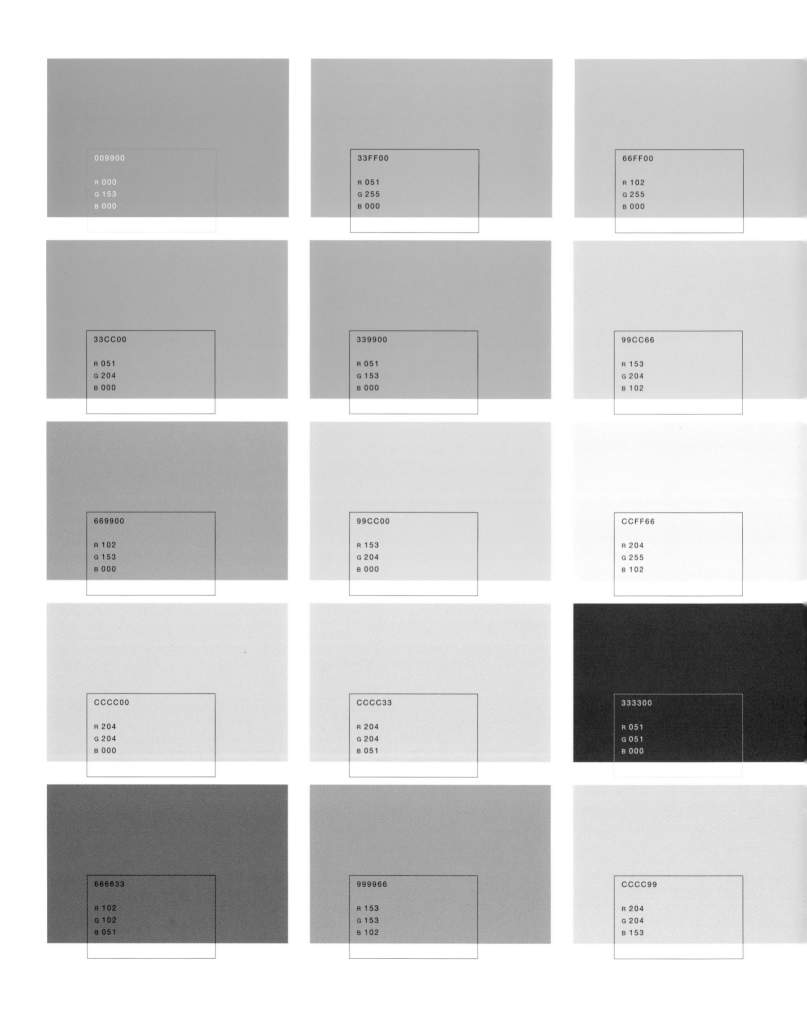

009900

R 000
G 153
B 000

33FF00

R 051
G 255
B 000

66FF00

R 102
G 255
B 000

33CC00

R 051
G 204
B 000

339900

R 051
G 153
B 000

99CC66

R 153
G 204
B 102

669900

R 102
G 153
B 000

99CC00

R 153
G 204
B 000

CCFF66

R 204
G 255
B 102

CCCC00

R 204
G 204
B 000

CCCC33

R 204
G 204
B 051

333300

R 051
G 051
B 000

666633

R 102
G 102
B 051

999966

R 153
G 153
B 102

CCCC99

R 204
G 204
B 153

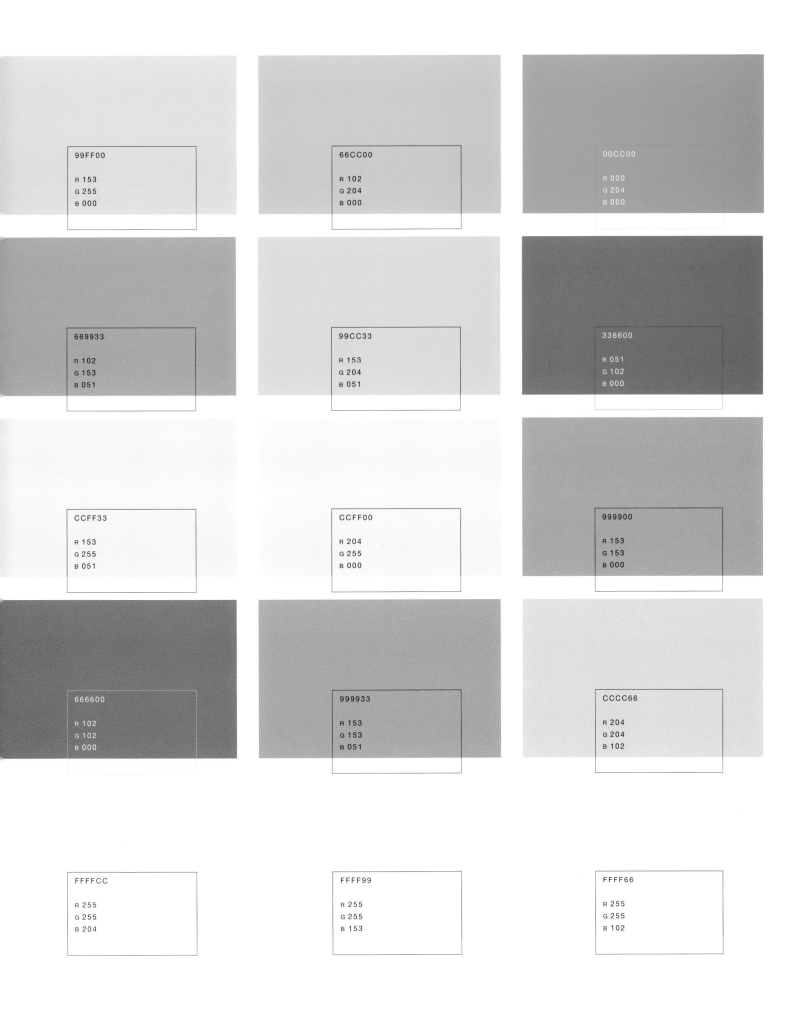

99FF00

R 153
G 255
B 000

66CC00

R 102
G 204
B 000

00CC00

R 000
G 204
B 000

669933

R 102
G 153
B 051

99CC33

R 153
G 204
B 051

336600

R 051
G 102
B 000

CCFF33

R 153
G 255
B 051

CCFF00

R 204
G 255
B 000

999900

R 153
G 153
B 000

666600

R 102
G 102
B 000

999933

R 153
G 153
B 051

CCCC66

R 204
G 204
B 102

FFFFCC

R 255
G 255
B 204

FFFF99

R 255
G 255
B 153

FFFF66

R 255
G 255
B 102

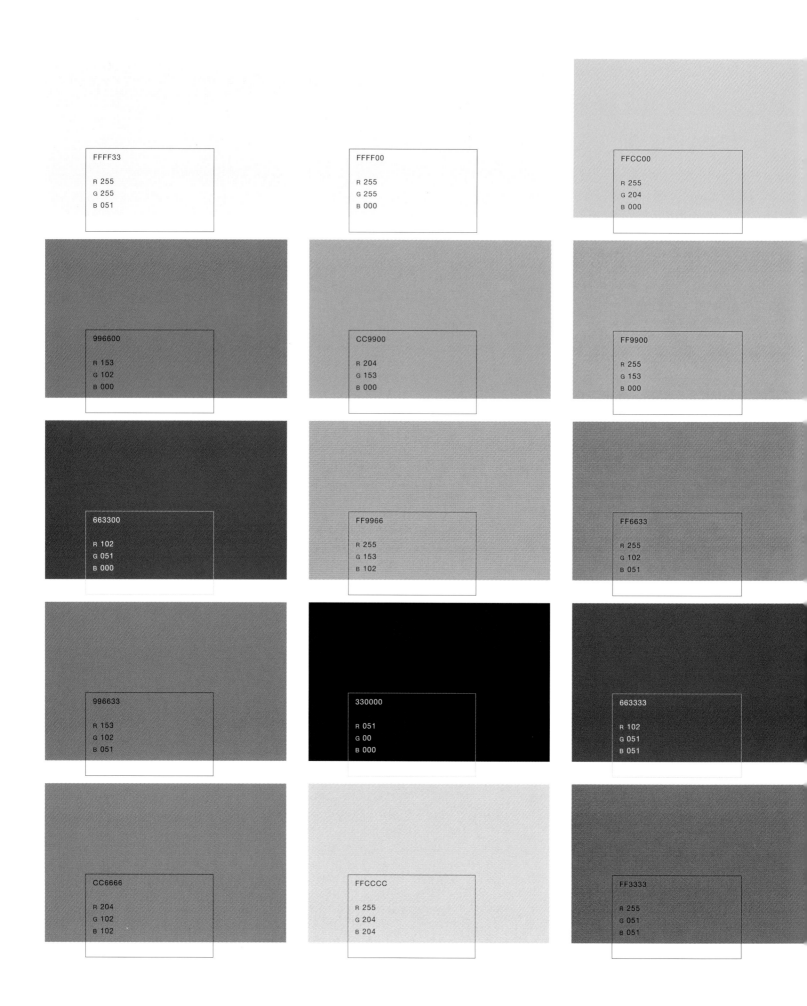

FFFF33

R 255
G 255
B 051

FFFF00

R 255
G 255
B 000

FFCC00

R 255
G 204
B 000

996600

R 153
G 102
B 000

CC9900

R 204
G 153
B 000

FF9900

R 255
G 153
B 000

663300

R 102
G 051
B 000

FF9966

R 255
G 153
B 102

FF6633

R 255
G 102
B 051

996633

R 153
G 102
B 051

330000

R 051
G 00
B 000

663333

R 102
G 051
B 051

CC6666

R 204
G 102
B 102

FFCCCC

R 255
G 204
B 204

FF3333

R 255
G 051
B 051

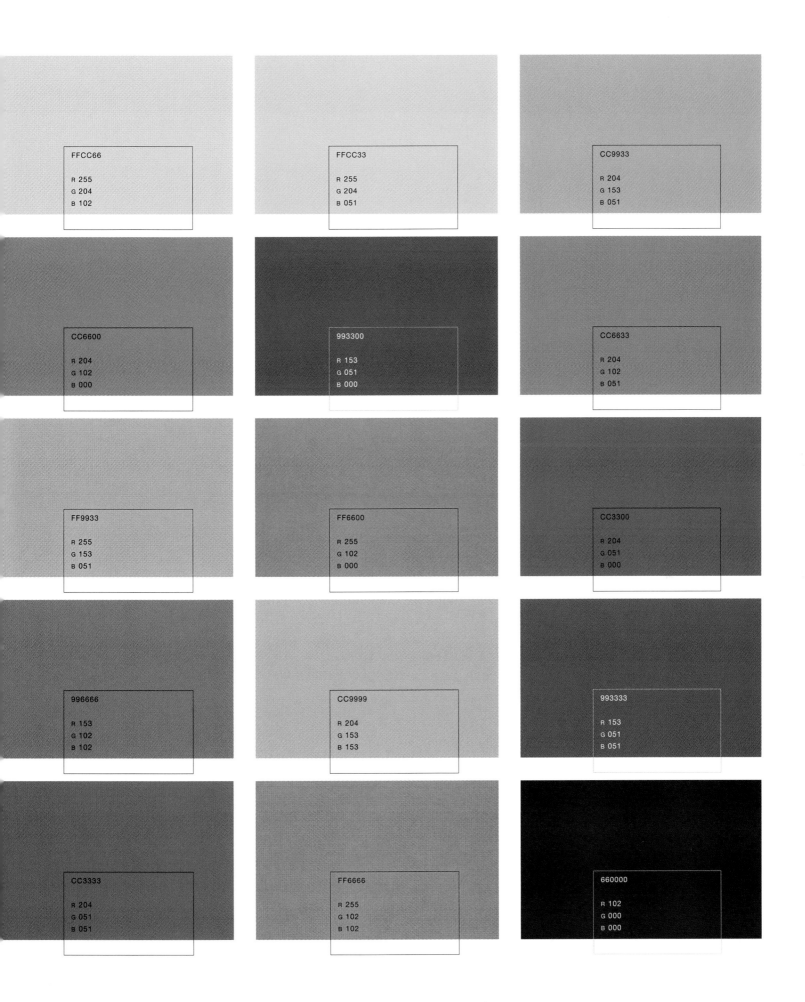

FFCC66

R 255
G 204
B 102

FFCC33

R 255
G 204
B 051

CC9933

R 204
G 153
B 051

CC6600

R 204
G 102
B 000

993300

R 153
G 051
B 000

CC6633

R 204
G 102
B 051

FF9933

R 255
G 153
B 051

FF6600

R 255
G 102
B 000

CC3300

R 204
G 051
B 000

996666

R 153
G 102
B 102

CC9999

R 204
G 153
B 153

993333

R 153
G 051
B 051

CC3333

R 204
G 051
B 051

FF6666

R 255
G 102
B 102

660000

R 102
G 000
B 000

1. Stick to the 216 Web-safe palette at all times.
2. Toss the palette out the window and use any color you want.

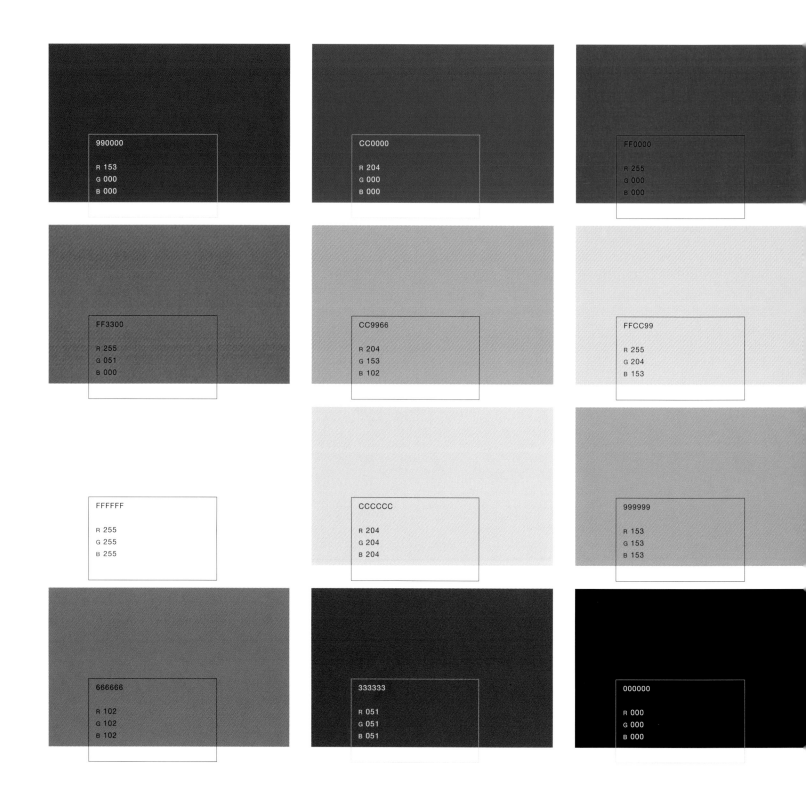

990000

R 153
G 000
B 000

CC0000

R 204
G 000
B 000

FF0000

R 255
G 000
B 000

FF3300

R 255
G 051
B 000

CC9966

R 204
G 153
B 102

FFCC99

R 255
G 204
B 153

FFFFFF

R 255
G 255
B 255

CCCCCC

R 204
G 204
B 204

999999

R 153
G 153
B 153

666666

R 102
G 102
B 102

333333

R 051
G 051
B 051

000000

R 000
G 000
B 000

Web designers complain all the time about the incredible restrictions the Web-safe palette imposes, and many times choose not to use colors from the 216 palette at all. Of course, there's a devil's advocate point of view here. Many print designers get excited at the fact that they can use that much color for free! Color processing in print is expensive, on the Web, it's not. So some designers feel empowered to have color to use at all.

But this doesn't answer the question as to how a designer really deals with this situation. In the real world of Web design, many designers don't even pay attention to the 216 Web-safe palette, much less the subtler yet still real concerns of even more limited palettes for true cross-platform, cross-browser color control.

Aside from tossing your hands up in utter despair, there are two routes you can take regarding Web-safe color.

1. Stick to the 216 Web-safe palette at all times.

2. Toss the palette out the window and use any color you want.

Now, depending upon your circumstances, either of these choices can be seen as wise or reckless.

A good example of this might be with Intranet applications. When you know the type of computers, browsers, and monitors the majority of your audience uses, you have much more flexibility in terms of color choice. If most people are accessing your pages with high-end browsers and monitors, here's an opportunity to work outside of the Web-safe palette.

However, if you have a global audience or one that might consist of high variables in the quality of computers in use, sticking to the Web-safe palette is wise.

The laughable fact is that even if you're extremely careful and use the 216 Web-safe palette, the variations between platforms, browsers, and monitor types will render your colors inconsistent.

VisiBone

Web Palette Color Distinction Test

Sat, 30 Jan 1999

Dear Webmasters and Designers,

Thanks very much for the careful responses to this survey from the Webdesign-L and VisiBone mailing lists. Here are the results, displayed somewhat crudely by operating system, which seemed about the only way to differentiate answers that mattered. I don't know if brands mean much any more (e.g., as heard on public radio, "Have you driven a Volvo lately?") but here are the monitors represented, almost as many brands as respondents.

- Gateway VX900
- Supermatch PressView
- NEC MultiSync XE21, XV17
- ViewSonic PT770, G810
- Apple multisync, trinitron
- Nokia
- IBM? 8515
- Sonica scandvision
- Dell Inspiron 3000
- Sony multi scan
- Compaq V70
- Impression TV
- Princeton Graphic Ultra

Here is the original question, reworded slightly so the answer tallies make sense. **"Do these four reds appear _different_ to you? If they don't, you'll see one wide red rectangle. If they do, you'll see four tall red rectangles up against one another."**

R	RRP	RRO	LHR
FF0000	FF0033	FF3300	FF3333

Obviously	Mac Mac Mac Mac NT Win95 Win98
Subtly	Mac Mac
Barely	NT Win95 Win95 Win95 Win95 Win95 Win98 Win98
Not at all	NT NT NT Win95 Win95 Win95 Win95 Win95 Win98

How about these four greens

G	GGT	GGS	LHG
00FF00	00FF33	33FF00	33FF33

Obviously	
Subtly	Mac
Barely	Mac Mac Mac Mac NT Win95 Win95 Win98
Not at all	NT NT NT NT Win95 Win95 Win95 Win95 Win95 Win95 Win98 Win98 Win95 Win95 Win98

Or these four blues

B	BBA	BBV	LHB
0000FF	0033FF	3300FF	3333FF

Obviously	Mac Mac Mac Mac Mac NT Win95 Win98
Subtly	Mac Win95 Win95 Win98 Win98
Barely	NT Win95 Win98
Not at all	NT NT NT Win95 Win95 Win95 Win95 Win95 Win98

And how about all these eight "blacks":

K	OWR	OWY	OWG	OWC	OWB	OWM	OG
000000	330000	333300	003300	003333	000033	330033	333333

Obviously	Mac Mac Mac Mac Mac NT NT NT Win95 Win95 Win95 Win98 Win98 Win98
Subtly	Win95 Win95 Win95 Win98 Win98
Barely	NT Win95
Not at all	NT Win95

For contrast, the following four shades of red should be obviously different to everybody

LHR	LRP	LRO	LFR
FF3333	FF3366	FF6633	FF6666

Clearly, Mac's tend to do a better job than PC's. No surprises there. But Mac's are not perfect either. See the greens: nobody reported they could see obvious distinctions among all of them.

One technical point on the differences between the answers in red, green and blue, and how it's easy to draw the precise, wrong conclusions. Note that the greens are much more likely to appear identical than reds or blues. That's not a crime in green representation, it's in red and blue. Notice that the green samples differ only in their red and blue values — the greens all use a green value of FF and red and blue values of 00 or 33. Several reported that within a set of four rectangles, some shades appeared identical while others did not. Based on all of this I conclude

- Green levels of 00 versus 33 are the most distinguishable by far
- Red less so
- Blue least of all

I tend to believe this distinction only represents eyeball physics, and that the crimes somewhere in the driver/monitor system are uniform across the three colors.

Summary

Now there are many aspects to this survey and the conclusions that would make a statistician blanche in horror. The sampling is from a unique group, with voluntary participation to boot. The questions and answers are terribly subjective. Maybe some big magazine with a big budget can do it "right" with representative samples and sensitive color test equipment. I'm certainly not able or willing. But here's a little data and here's where I think it points.

It's apparent there is some seriously, widespread nonlinearity on the way from the numbers to the eyeballs among the low (dim) values in the 216 color web-safe palette. The results of this survey imply that choosing between 00 and 33 for RGB color codes will make a less than obvious difference for 70% of the people who view them. For 40%, there will be no difference at all. I still don't have anything in the way of an explanation for this bizarre state of affairs. I'm sure there's an engineer or two somewhere who's responsible. If anyone has clues, please let me know.

When I design a web site I certainly can't afford to ignore a random 40% of the users. Until monitor technology is much more advanced, or unless the audience is anything other than captive and homogenous, I suggest we're in a disappointing situation. **We really only have 125 colors to choose from.**

2.31

VisiBone test

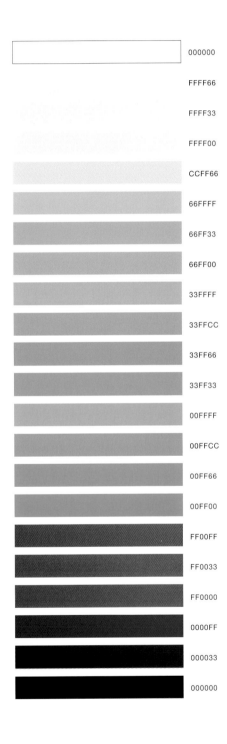

000000

FFFF66

FFFF33

FFFF00

CCFF66

66FFFF

66FF33

66FF00

33FFFF

33FFCC

33FF66

33FF33

00FFFF

00FFCC

00FF66

00FF00

FF00FF

FF0033

FF0000

0000FF

000033

000000

2.32
WebMonkey test,
only 22 colors

Once you've determined whether or not to use Web-safe color, it's time to turn your attention to writing that color within your Web documents. Yes, there are certain methodologies that will be employed for graphics, but I'll discuss those in Chapter 3. Right now, the focus is on how color is written and then interpreted by the Web browser.

There are three ways of marking up Web color. The first is the use of hexadecimal color in a standard HTML or XHTML document. In this case, RGB color is converted to hexadecimal (base 16) values and used along with attributes to achieve color. Note that hexadecimal values can be Web-safe, or not.

The second way is to use color names in the same way that you would hexadecimal color—as the value of an attribute name. There are 16 color names legally reserved for use in HTML 4.01, and there are 126 color names that have been introduced by browsers and offer a wider range of color. However, these colors are not considered standard and will not necessarily be supported by all browsers.

Finally, in Cascading Style Sheets, you can use hexadecimal color, color names, or RGB values themselves. I'll show you how to do each of these things. But first, I'm going to explain how you can convert RGB values to hex values.

Hexadecimal is the base 16 number system, which consists of numbers 0–15 and the letters A–F. A byte (8 bits) can be represented using two hexadecimal characters, which make any combination of binary information less cumbersome to understand. In relation to Web color, hexadecimal values *always* appear with six characters.

You can find the hexadecimal value of any color on your own by using a scientific calculator and a drawing program such as Photoshop. In Photoshop, pass your cursor over any color. The "info" dialog will display the individual red, green, and blue values of the color in the form of numbers (figure 2.33). Simply enter each of the values into the scientific calculator—one color at a time (red value first, and so forth). Switch to "hex." The scientific calculator will then give you an alphanumeric or numeric combination for the corresponding color value (Figure 2.34).

So let's say I have a deep red color as shown in Figure 2.33. The red value in my example is 204, the hexadecimal value is CC. Now I'll complete the same process for the green and blue values. You should always end up with a total of six characters. The result of my RGB-to-hexadecimal conversion for the red color is: CC0000. Different colors will get different combinations, some with all the same numeric values, others in pairs, such as "CC9900."

As you might have noticed, 0 for a red, green, or blue value is going to be written as 00.

Here are some helpful websites that provide conversion tools and charts:

Color Center, http://www.hidaho.com/colorcenter/cc.html
Lynda.com, http://www.lynda.com/
Visibone, http://www.visibone.com/

Bear in mind that you still must understand the safe palette issue in order to use most online converters. They are paying attention to a broad-spectrum palette, not necessarily a safe one.

Newer versions of Photoshop, Illustrator, and many other popular image editing programs have Web-safe hex information already built in. But even in these editors you'll need to use a scientific calculator or other tool to work with colors outside the Web-safe palette.

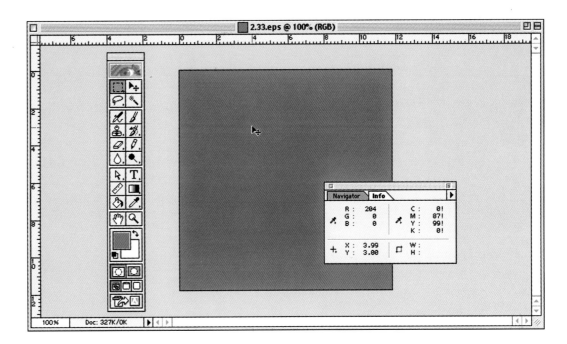

2.33

RGB information in Photoshop

2.34

Scientific calculator in Windows

Adding Color using HTML and XHTML   *Great Body, Baby*

Web authors can use standard HTML or XHTML to achieve color effects. The HTML 4.0 recommendation, however, considers color-related to be presentation. As such, Cascading Style Sheets (CSS) are favored. However, due to cross-browser, cross-platform problems with CSS, many authors still write color directly into their documents. It's perfectly fine to do this in HTML or XHTML documents that fall into the transitional Document Type Definitions for each. More details on this can be found in my books, Special Edition Using HTML 4.0, Sixth Edition, and Special Edition Using XHTML, both from Que Publishing. You may also wish to visit the World Wide Web Consortium, responsible for publishing Web mark-up recommendations, at www.w3.org/.

The most immediate application of color is found within the HTML and XHTML <body> tag, or CSS BODY: element, where you can define backgrounds, text, and link styles. You can also use color in table cell backgrounds and, using style sheets, you can put color in almost any logical place, such as behind text, or as a backdrop for a given paragraph.

The body tag allows for the following color attributes:

`bgcolor="x"`. This value in hex argues the background color of the entire page.

`text="x"`. The text argument creates the color for all standard, non-linked text on the page.

`link="x"`. The color entered here will appear wherever you've linked text.

`vlink="x"`. A visited link will appear in this color.

`alink="x"`. An active link—one that is in the process of being clicked, will appear in the color you argue for here.

A <body> tag with these attributes appears as follows. You'll note that I've simply placed a hexadecimal value into the attribute value field. I begin each individual attribute value with the "#" sign:

```
<body bgcolor="#000000" text="#CCCCCC" link="#CCCC00"
vlink="#3300FF" alink="#CC33CC">
```

Figure 2.35 shows the results.

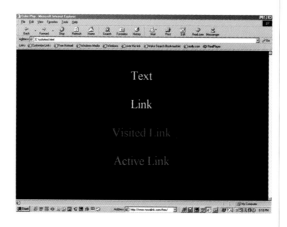

2.35

HTML and hex colors create the colors on this page

Other areas where color can be applied without using style sheets include fonts:

`<font color="#CCFFCC">Hello!</font>`

and table cell backgrounds:

`<td bgcolor="#3366FF">This cell now has a background color</td>`

You may decide to use a background graphic on your page, in which case you will use the background="url" argument within the above string. This alerts the browser to load the graphic from the location specified. If you're using a background graphic, I highly recommend including a background color attribute as well. This way your background color will load instantly, and your graphic will then load over that color. The end product is less jarring and creates a cohesive visual effect.

Some of you might have seen HTML color attributes that use the name of the color rather than the hex value: <body bgcolor="red" text="white" link="yellow" vlink="green">.

As mentioned, there are two primary sets of color names: those that are considered standard (fit in with a World Wide Web Consortium recommendation), and those that are browser-specific. What's interesting about both sets of named colors is that they are not all part of the 216 Web-safe palette!

The standardized palette can be seen in Figure 2.36, and the color names can be seen in Figure 2.37. Once again, it's very important to mention that using color names from the non-standard spectrum may not work properly across browsers. As such, it's in your best interest to stick with hex numbers or standard color names.

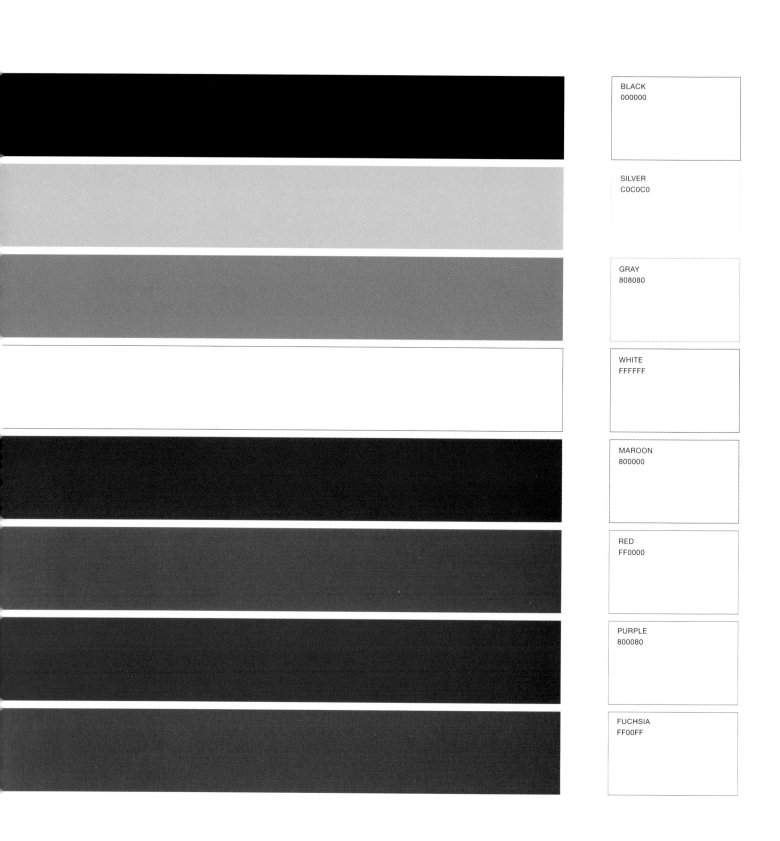

BLACK
000000

SILVER
C0C0C0

GRAY
808080

WHITE
FFFFFF

MAROON
800000

RED
FF0000

PURPLE
800080

FUCHSIA
FF00FF

2.36

The 16 color names
in HTML 4.01

GREEN
008000

LIME
00FF00

OLIVE
808000

YELLOW
FFFF00

NAVY
000080

BLUE
0000FF

TEAL
008080

AQUA
00FFFF

2.37
Browser-specific color names
(NB: color names often appear
random in print, check on screen
to ensure consistant results)

WHITE
FFFFFF

RED
FF0000

ORANGE
FFA500

YELLOW
FFFF00

GREEN
008000

BLUE
0000FF

PURPLE
800080

BLACK
000000

ALICE BLUE A0CE00	
ANTIQUE WHITE FAEBD7	
AQUA 00FFFF	
AQUAMARINE 7FFFD4	
AZUR F0FFFF	
BIEGE F5F5DC	
BISQUE FFE4C4	
BLEACHED ALMOND FFEBCD	

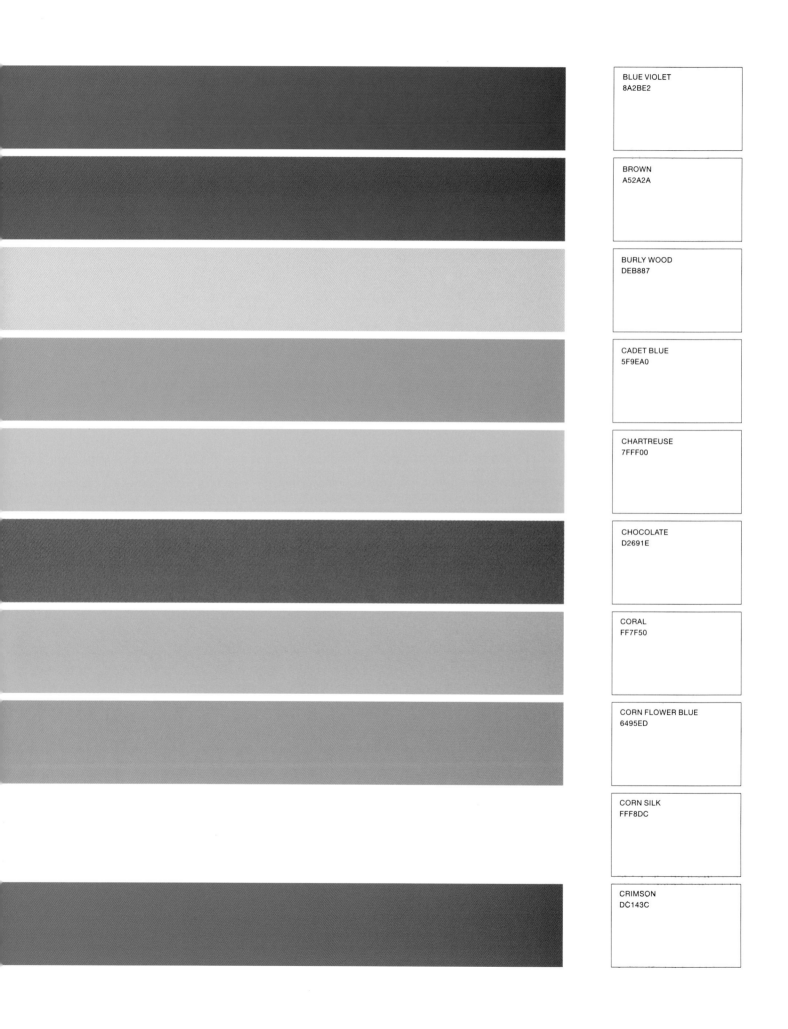

BLUE VIOLET
8A2BE2

BROWN
A52A2A

BURLY WOOD
DEB887

CADET BLUE
5F9EA0

CHARTREUSE
7FFF00

CHOCOLATE
D2691E

CORAL
FF7F50

CORN FLOWER BLUE
6495ED

CORN SILK
FFF8DC

CRIMSON
DC143C

CYAN
00FFFF

DARK BLUE
00008B

DARK CYAN
008B8B

DARK GOLDENROD
B8860B

DARK GRAY
A9A9A9

DARK GREEN
006400

DARK KHAKI
BDB76B

DARK MAGENTA
BD008B

DARK OLIVE GREEN
556B2F

DARK ORANGE
FF8C00

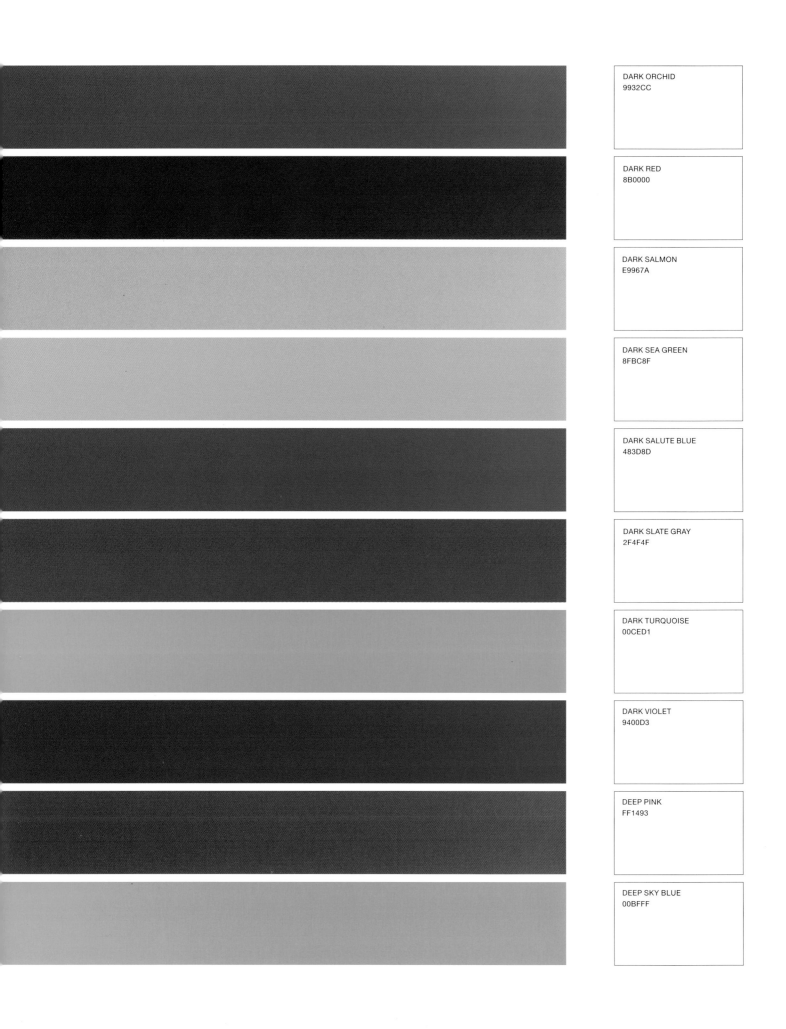

DARK ORCHID
9932CC

DARK RED
8B0000

DARK SALMON
E9967A

DARK SEA GREEN
8FBC8F

DARK SALUTE BLUE
483D8D

DARK SLATE GRAY
2F4F4F

DARK TURQUOISE
00CED1

DARK VIOLET
9400D3

DEEP PINK
FF1493

DEEP SKY BLUE
00BFFF

DIM GRAY 696969	
DODGER BLUE 1E90FF	
FIRE BRICK B22222	
FLORAL WHITE FFFAF0	
FOREST GREEN 228B22	
FUSCHIA FF00FF	
GAINSBORO DCDCDC	
GHOST WHITE F8F8FF	
GOLD FFD700	
GOLDENROD DAA520	

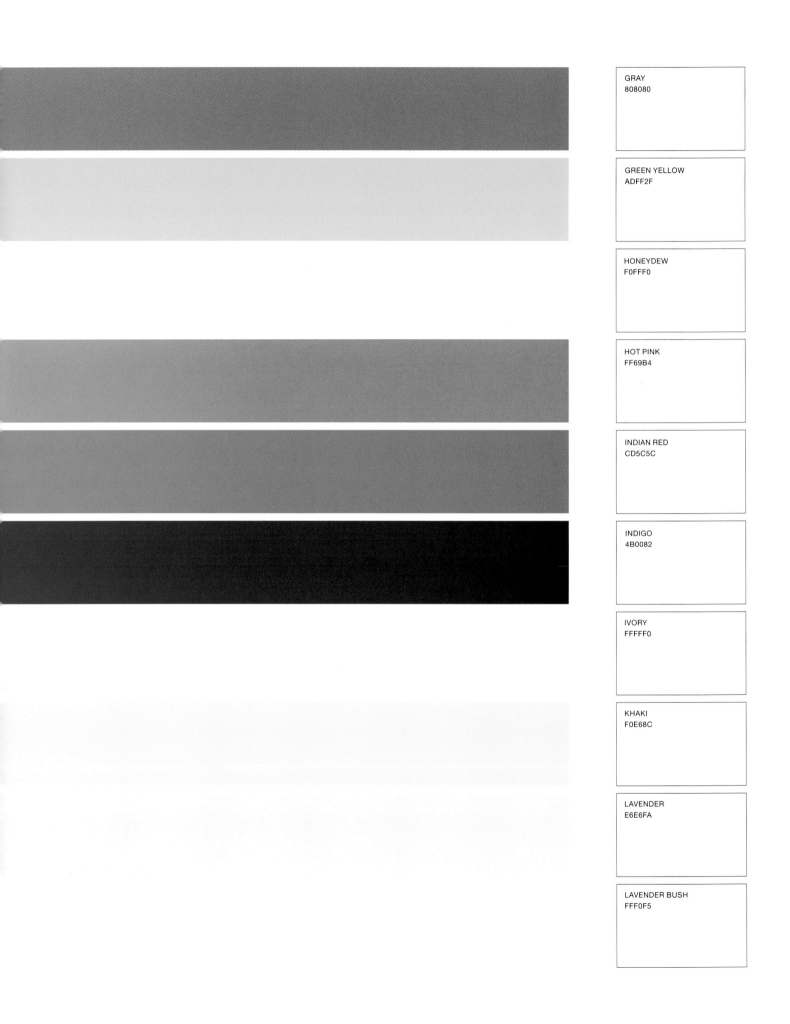

GRAY
808080

GREEN YELLOW
ADFF2F

HONEYDEW
F0FFF0

HOT PINK
FF69B4

INDIAN RED
CD5C5C

INDIGO
4B0082

IVORY
FFFFF0

KHAKI
F0E68C

LAVENDER
E6E6FA

LAVENDER BUSH
FFF0F5

LEMON CHIFFON
FFFACD

LIGHT BLUE
ADD8E6

LIGHT CORAL
F08080

LIGHT CYAN
E0FFFF

LIGHT GOLDENROD YELLOW
FAFAD2

LIGHT GREEN
90EE90

LIGHT GRAY
D3D3D3

LIGHT PINK
FFB6C1

LIGHT SALMON
FFA07A

LIGHT SEA GREEN
21B2AA

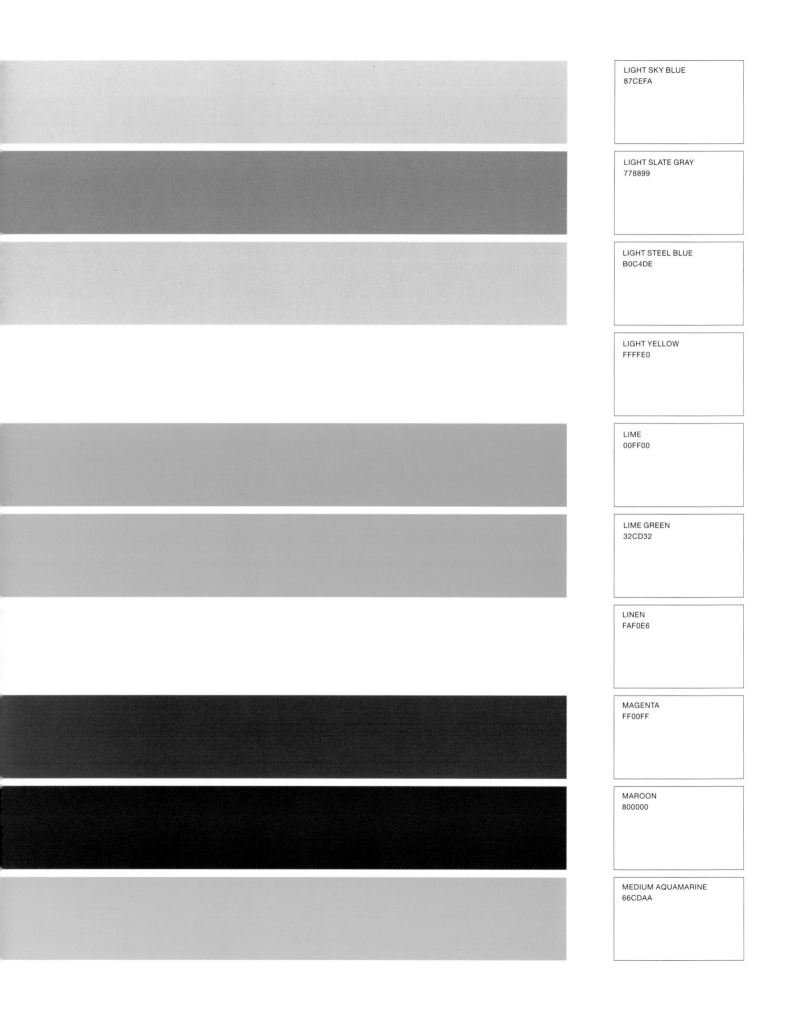

LIGHT SKY BLUE
87CEFA

LIGHT SLATE GRAY
778899

LIGHT STEEL BLUE
B0C4DE

LIGHT YELLOW
FFFFE0

LIME
00FF00

LIME GREEN
32CD32

LINEN
FAF0E6

MAGENTA
FF00FF

MAROON
800000

MEDIUM AQUAMARINE
66CDAA

MEDIUM BLUE
0000CD

MEDIUM ORCHID
BA55D3

MEDIUM PURPLE
9370DB

MEDIUM SEA GREEN
3CB371

MEDIUM SLATE BLUE
7B68EE

MEDIUM SPRING GREEN
00FA9A

MEDIUM TURQUOISE
48D1CC

MEDIUM VIOLET RED
C71585

MIDNIGHT BLUE
191970

MINT CREAM
F5FFFA

MISTY ROSE
FFE4E1

NAVAJO WHITE
FFDEAD

NAVY
000080

OLD LACE
FDF5E6

OLIVE
808000

OLIVE DRAB
6B8E23

ORANGE RED
FF4500

ORCHID
DA70D6

PALE GOLDENROD
EEE8AA

PALE GREEN
98FB98

PALE TURQUOISE
AFEEEE

PALE VIOLET RED
DB7093

PAPAYA WHIP
FFEFD5

PEACH PUFF
FFDAB9

PERU
CD853F

PINK
FFC0CB

PLUM
DDA0DD

POWDER BLUE
B0E0E6

ROSY BROWN
BC8F8F

ROYAL BLUE
4169E1

SADDLE BROWN
8B4513

SEA GREEN
2E8B57

SEA SHELL
FFF5EE

SIENNA
A0522D

SILVER
C0C0C0

SKY BLUE
87CEEB

SLATE BLUE
6A5ACD

SLATE GRAY
708090

SNOW
FFFAFA

SPRING GREEN
00FF7F

STEEL BLUE
4682B4

TAN
D2B486

TEAL
008080

THISTLE
D8BFDB

TOMATO
FF6347

TURQUOISE
40E0D0

VIOLET
EE82EE

WHEAT
F5DEB3

WHITE SMOKE
F5F5F5

YELLOW GREEN
9ACD32

Color with Style Sheets

Those readers who keep up with changes to Web mark-up languages are familiar with the fact that all color codes as mentioned in the previous section are considered deprecated. This means that using color in element attributes is not recommended. Instead, Cascading Style Sheets are supposed to be used.

But, there are problems with CSS in that many browsers don't properly support them. So, as a designer you're left weighing the all-important decision whether to follow the standard recommendations or to do what you need to do to make a website work.

Personally, I'm very concerned with W3C recommendations. I believe that following them is ideologically important because it encourages Web designers, browser developers, and software companies building visual editing tools for the Web to conform to a set of rules. The advantages to this are many—not least of which is that with such rules we won't have to struggle for cross-browser, cross-platform consistency.

But until that hope is realized, we are challenged to find balance. And since we're working in the real Web world, the goal is to somehow balance what is recommended and what works. To that end, many designers find that combining style sheets with a transitional HTML 4.01 or XHTML 1.0 mark-up using color attributes in places where there might be cross-browser conflicts is the perfect solution. Yes, it requires a bit more study, but the results are going to be a lot more satisfactory.

Here's a sample external style sheet for the background, text, and link color using hex:

```
BODY {background: #FFFFFF; color: #000000;}
A {color: #CCCCCC; }
```

There aren't style sheet standard methods for calling on visited or active links. *Pseudo-classes* appear in the style sheet literature to achieve this, but you should test them before use: A.link, A.visited, A.active. Here's a sample using color names:

```
A.visited {purple;}
A.active {red;}
```

Style can also be used inline to enhance individual pieces of text, using hex that is not Web-safe:

```
<span style="color: #800000; background: #808000">Colorful Me!</span>
```

If you'd like to create a backdrop for a complete paragraph, you can also use style. In this case, I've used inline style with RGB values instead of hex or color names:

```
<p style="background: 204, 51, 51">
"Love nothing but that which comes to you in the pattern of your destiny." –Marcus Aurelius.</p>
```

As you can see, I put the red value first, the green value second, and the blue value third, separated by commas. This is a perfectly acceptable way to add color to style sheets.

For more information on style sheets, I'd like to recommend you to an excellent online resource edited by Eric A. Meyer. He's a member of the W3C working committee on CSS, and he's prepared a very comprehensive set of charts that show how various CSS properties are supported by various browsers. Please see http://style.webreview.com/ for more information.

With these examples, you can get a glimpse at how style sheets can be very powerful design tools—a great deal of information can be packed into them, easing up on the amount of resulting HTML or XHTML elements and attributes, and conforming with the ideology of separation of presentation and formatting as found in Web mark-up. However, as mentioned throughout this book, following recommendations—while certainly encouraged—can also be limited by browser technology and distribution issues.

Creating Individual Palettes

Whenever I'm working on a site, I like to map out the site's individual color palette. I select any HTML-based background colors, text colors, link colors that I'll want to use. Color selections for a specific site are drawn from knowledge of the audience, the subject matter, and the client's desires. Keep in mind that color also communicates emotion and has cultural meanings (see Chapter 4), so build your palettes with any relevant concerns in mind.

A corporate website is going to have a distinctly different individual color palette than a more entertainment-oriented site. Going back to the earlier lesson on color, a corporate site is going to look for a harmonious scheme, with pleasing, calming colors. An entertainment site might enjoy bolder use of color, including subtractive primaries—yellow, blue, and red.

My own website, www.Molly.com, uses bright colors to create a warm and vibrant look. Table 2.1 shows the colors I've used on the site along with the RGB and hex values. Note that these are all Web-safe colors.

I also create a swatch file of these colors so I can pull from them when I'm working in Illustrator or Photoshop. Figure 2.39 shows my palette.

This information comes in very handy when I need to make updates or changes. Web designers should create a cataloging system as it will help to keep site information in order, and available for future reference.

Table 2.1: www.Molly.Com Individual Palette Reference

Color	RGB Value	Hexadecimal Value
Black	000	000000
White	255, 255, 255	FFFFFF
Orange	255, 153, 0	FF9900
Lime	153, 204, 0	99CC00
Rich Yellow	255, 204, 51	FFCC33

2.39

Individual site palette

molly
author INSTRUCTOR WEB designer

Featured Book

Special Edition Using
XHTML is in bookstores
now!

Quick Email Link

Q: What's this Web site for?

A: This Web site showcases my work and thoughts. Think of it as a personality site. Given that, one hopes I have an interesting enough personality to keep you entertained for at least a little while.

- recent photos
- Famous People I Know

MOLLY'S DAILY BLOG

Sunday, March 25, 2001

san francisco hotel rooom i can see
the tender . . . loin I can hear
blues harps players in the streets
playing better than the guy
who hangs around on fridays

No matter the clouds
san francisco burns off of me
like a lifetime of marine layers

I get my lovers confused
but never my loves, no.

I always know who you guys are.

See, to take the heart

Moving Toward Images

Of course, color is inherent in images, too. And while much of the technology in terms of bits and color display concerns carry over to images, there are unique challenges when it comes to preserving and gaining effective color with images. In Chapter 3, we'll take a close look at those challenges, and learn via a balance of technology and practical application how to get the very best color and quality from the images we use on the Web.

WEB COLOR
AND IMAGES

Chapter Three

. . . there is no reason not to set your sights on graphics that are rich in color, clear and crisp, and still have reasonable download times.

Web Color and Images

Web Graphic Philosophy

Images comprise much of the color found on the Web. But achieving color precision and consistency with graphics can be difficult. Part of the problems with consistent graphic quality lie in the issues I've already discussed in this book: hardware inconsistencies, platform and operating system differences, browser version variables. Another area of challenge lies with the abundant misperceptions about how graphics should be chosen, processed, used, and optimized.

You might be a seasoned graphic designer, or a novice simply interested in a quality look. Either way, there is no reason not to set your sights on graphics that are rich in color, clear and crisp, and still have reasonable download times. The output of a successful Web graphic balances esthetics and speed.

If you're looking to create graphics for general Web audiences, you must take download times into account. A relationship exists between browsers and servers—the browser, via the Web mark-up syntax that asks for a given graphic, requests that graphic from the server. The graphic must then send its binary data over the connection available. In some cases, that connection will be very fast—broadband access such as cable and DSL are very common in people's homes now. T1 and even T3 access are common in business and industry. But, for a variety of reasons, slower modem connections abound.

Designing richly colored graphics for the Web typically means you have to make some very specific decisions about how you're going to use graphics on your pages. Overloading a page doesn't make sense. Creating very weighty graphics can also be problematic. The goal is to learn to plan your pages, and combine that smart planning with technical know-how to get the most (or the least, as the case may be) out of your graphics. The sacrifice of visual quality is not necessary if careful selection, optimization, and proper sizing and layout of Web graphics on a page is fully considered.

As you become more familiar with Web color, and how you can use it on the Web, you'll see that relying on browser-based color for backgrounds, text, and links can create a rich environment where graphics might hardly be needed at all (Figure 3.1).

By starting with a base understanding of color use, graphics can then be used to enhance and extend a design, rather than to be the design's core.

Resources

action
mission
members
resources

Educational F.A.Q. General CSS EcmaScript DOM, "DHTML"

An expanding directory of sites that can help you make sense of the standards, and prepare you for things that go wrong. If you're new to the world of CSS, XML, and so on, you'll also find our new Educational F.A.Q. extremely helpful.

General

The Motherlode. Includes W3C info, the W3C Validator and mailing list, resources for HTML help, usability and more.

Cascading Style Sheets

CSS separates markup from content, and that's a good thing. Stay in style with our selected resources on the evolving spec, support issues, and bugs.

ECMAScript, son of Javascript

Everything you ever wanted to know about ECMAScript (and Javascript) but were afraid to ask. Including the ECMAScript definition, differences from Javascript (and Jscript), bugs, and incompatibilities.

DOM, Platform Issues & Cross-Browser DHTML

The W3C DOM, useful studies on differences between Explorer and Navigator, Mozilla New Layout, writing DHTML for all browsers, and much more.

More

Suggest a resource.
Send us the URL, the name, and a brief description. Thanks!

3.1

Web Standards Project
(WaSP: rich color, few graphics)

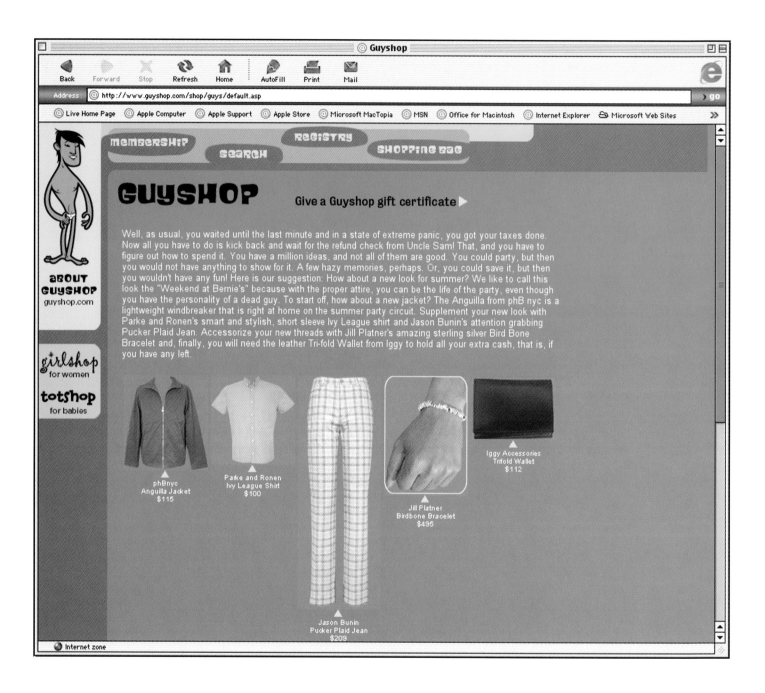

@ Guyshop

Back Forward Stop Refresh Home AutoFill Print Mail

Address: @ http://www.guyshop.com/shop/guys/default.asp > go

@ Live Home Page @ Apple Computer @ Apple Support @ Apple Store @ Microsoft MacTopia @ MSN @ Office for Macintosh @ Internet Explorer @ Microsoft Web Sites »

MEMBERSHIP   SEARCH   REGISTRY   SHOPPING BAG

ABOUT GUYSHOP
guyshop.com

girlshop for women

totshop for babies

GUYSHOP

Give a Guyshop gift certificate ▶

Well, as usual, you waited until the last minute and in a state of extreme panic, you got your taxes done. Now all you have to do is kick back and wait for the refund check from Uncle Sam! That, and you have to figure out how to spend it. You have a million ideas, and not all of them are good. You could party, but then you would not have anything to show for it. A few hazy memories, perhaps. Or, you could save it, but then you wouldn't have any fun! Here is our suggestion: How about a new look for summer? We like to call this look the "Weekend at Bernie's" because with the proper attire, you can be the life of the party, even though you have the personality of a dead guy. To start off, how about a new jacket? The Anguilla from phB nyc is a lightweight windbreaker that is right at home on the summer party circuit. Supplement your new look with Parke and Ronen's smart and stylish, short sleeve Ivy League shirt and Jason Bunin's attention grabbing Pucker Plaid Jean. Accessorize your new threads with Jill Platner's amazing sterling silver Bird Bone Bracelet and, finally, you will need the leather Tri-fold Wallet from Iggy to hold all your extra cash, that is, if you have any left.

phBnyc
Anguilla Jacket
$115

Parke and Ronen
Ivy League Shirt
$100

Jason Bunin
Pucker Plaid Jean
$209

Jill Platner
Birdbone Bracelet
$495

Iggy Accessories
Trifold Wallet
$112

Internet zone

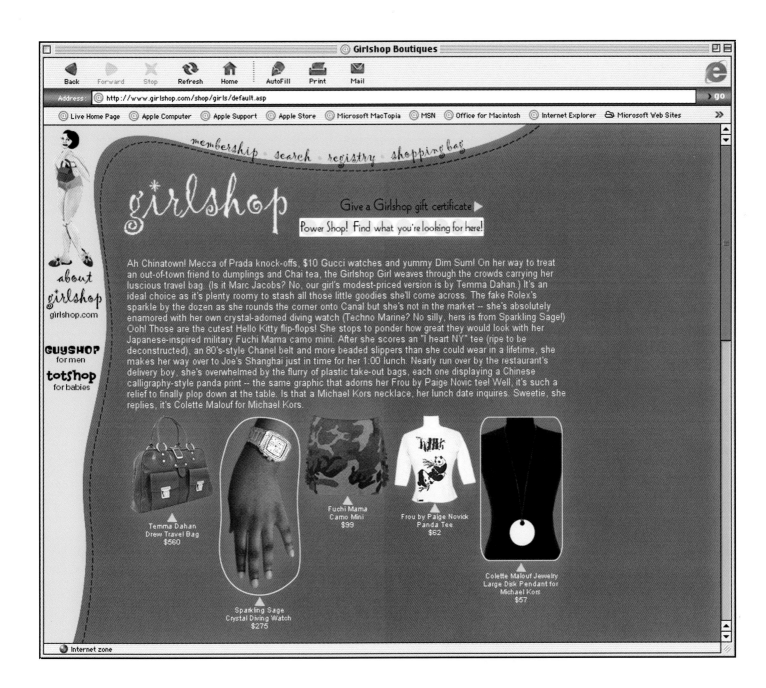

Graphic Basics

Computer graphics can be categorized in two primary ways: vector images and raster images. Each kind of image has a distinctive look and feel, as well as unique methods for editing and utilizing the image.

By mastering the basics of both types of computer-generated art and the software tools which can produce that art, you will have acquired a marketable skill that enables you to produce almost any graphic element imaginable.

Vector graphics are mathematically-calculated images. Vector graphics consist of a series of lines and curves used to form different shapes. Each line and curve is generated using a mathematical instruction which provides the beginning, ending, and path of the line or curve.

Vector graphics are very easy to scale because it is simply a process of altering the mathematical equations involved in the image. If you save a vector graphic in its native format using a vector graphic program, such as Adobe Illustrator, you can later modify that file to make the graphic larger or smaller without losing quality or increasing file size.

Vector art is composed of Bezier curves. Bezier curves define shapes or objects through the positioning of two anchor points, a segment, two direction lines, and two direction handles. Direction lines define the direction of a curve. It makes sense that straight paths or sharp corners do not have direction lines.

Bezier curves were first introduced to the European automobile industry in the 1960s for the purpose of maintaining the integrity of drawings during the design process. The mainstream drawing programs for computers at the time were pixel-based.

Pixel-based programs produced results with stair-stepped pixelated lines and shapes. This can result in jagged edges (this is known by a very serious technical term: *jaggies*).

Adobe Illustrator, released in 1988, was the first vector-based computer program to be made available to the general public. Illustrator allowed artists to draw hard-edged graphics on a computer and print out an image composed of clean, sharp lines and edges.

This advance was not only valuable for illustrators but also for typographers. Type fonts could be rendered using the same technology, enabling typographers to design hundreds of new fonts with ease.

Vector Image Tools

In order to create vector illustration, special tools have been developed that can make the calculations and save the digital data to a vector file format.

Several software products exist that emphasize vector graphic design, including:

Adobe Illustrator
This extremely popular drawing tool for Mac and Windows allows you to create vector art
www.adobe.com/products/illustrator/main.html**.**

Macromedia Freehand
Also available for Mac and Windows, Freehand information can be found at
www.macromedia.com/software/freehand/

Corel Draw
This drawing tool has historically been used on Windows platform machines, although Mac versions are available too
www.corel.com/draw9/draw9.htm**.**

Vector applications are especially good for the creation of illustrations with lots of curves, hard-edged shapes, and smooth lines. Graphic designers usually use these programs to design logos and to draw complex digital drawings. Vector applications are also used for technical drawings that can benefit from the sizing flexibility that vector formats offer.

Vector software is also an excellent choice for the creation of special effects. Vector art does not appear on the Web in its original format. With the exception of Adobe Acrobat Portable Document Files (PDF) and Flash files, all images that appear on the Web are pixel-based raster images. For a vector image to be positioned as a Web graphic, it must first be converted by saving or exporting it to JPEG or GIF.

An image created in a vector application can be exported as a raster file directly. Or, it may be saved to the native vector file format or to the cross-platform, cross-program vector EPS format. You can then open the file in another application such as Photoshop for image enhancement and the application of special effects.

If the other application is not object-oriented (as is the case with Photoshop) the image will automatically be *rasterized*. This is the conversion of vector to bitmap information for editing in the raster environment. Any further changes to the image will affect file size and appearance.

Adobe Illustrator is considered the professional standard for drawing programs

Macromedia Freehand is integrated into the Macromedia suite of Web graphic design tools

Corel Draw has been a popular desktop publishing program for Windows for many years. Corel has recently added a range of Web production tools to its software

Raster Art

It's likely you are already familiar with raster graphics types, which include the common Web file formats GIF and JPEG. In order to be viewable across multiple platforms and Web browsers, vector files must be rasterized to one of these common file formats.

Raster graphics (also referred to as *bitmapped* graphics) use the x/y axis to create a pre-defined grid of information about each pixel of the image. Pixels are the basic physical unit of an image. As you've already seen, pixels are individual tiles of colored light set up on a grid to form a mosaic. The pixels are so small that when the eye sees them, it blends them together to create a photographic image.

Each pixel in the grid is stored with color and other information. This limits how the file can be modified in terms of size because changes to the image involve changes to the pixels within the grid. You can make an image smaller without losing quality. But as you increase the size of your image, the number of pixels increases, thereby increasing file size. Also, as you increase the size of your image, each bit is stretched out to cover a larger number of pixels, resulting in blurry graphics.

Raster art is produced in raster programs. Raster programs manipulate bitmaps, which as described are a patterned mosaic of pixels containing digital information.

Popular raster applications include:

Adobe Photoshop
The emperor of professional digital design software
www.adobe.com/products/photoshop/main.html.

Corel Photo-Paint
Corel's raster companion to Draw
www.corel.com/paint9/index.htm.

Jasc Paint Shop Pro
Extremely popular among enthusiasts, PSP is a cost-effective alternative to high-priced professional programs
www.jasc.com/psp6/

If you want to be competitive, professional, and hirable as a Web graphic production specialist or designer, you've simply got to have Photoshop skills.

Adobe Photoshop is considered the professional standard for imaging software

Corel Photo-Paint is popular with some desktop publishing specialists

Jasc Paint Shop Pro is an extremely popular and affordable imaging program for Web enthusiasts

Exploring General File Types

As you dig deeper into the world of Web graphics, you'll be exposed to a number of file types. Some are specific to the Web, some are not. However, it's great to understand the most common file types—even if you won't be using them specifically for the Web. Often, certain kinds of files are used to exchange information between designers who will then convert the files into Web-based formats.

I'll cover Web-specific file formats later in the chapter, but I want to be sure to give you a bit of background into some general graphic file types.

Table 3.1—Common File Types		
File Acronym	**File Name**	**Description**
AI	Adobe Illustrator File	Native vector format for Adobe Illustrator Preserves color well
BMP	Windows Bitmap	Raster format for Windows Limits color
EPS	Encapsulated Postscript	Uncompressed vector and raster format
PCX	PC Paintbrush File	Raster format for Windows Preserves color moderately well
PDF	Portable Document Format	Vector format, read by Adobe Acrobat Preserves color well
PSD	Photoshop Document	Raster format that allows the retention of layers Preserves color well if not flattened
TIFF	Tagged Image File Format	Widely used Raster format Preserves colors quite well

Note that this isn't a comprehensive list of computer graphic file types. I have picked the ones that most people interested in Web graphic design are likely to come across at some point.

The Nitty and the Gritty: Web File Formats

Along with the general computer graphic file types introduced in the last section, there are a number of files specifically suited to the Web. We'll examine each type in detail. First, I'd like to discuss some of the general features of Web formats.

The two most commonly used Web graphic formats are the familiar GIF and JPEG, although a great deal of interest has been placed in a relative newcomer to the Web scene, the PNG. Of important note to the designer are Flash file formats (SWF), and an XML-based technology known as Scalable Vector Graphics (SVG). For our purposes, we're going to focus mostly on GIF and JPEG. However, I will give you some information and resources on other file formats should you be interested in finding out more about them.

There are advantages and disadvantages to every Web file format. Which format to save an image to is going to depend on the nature of the image itself and what you intend to do with it. Making the right choice will greatly influence the quality of your final image and as a result, your website as a whole.

As I mentioned before, in order for your images to load quickly, it is necessary for them to be compressed or reduced in bit-depth. Compression is the act of minimizing a file's weight by taking out certain digital information. Modifying bit-depth means reducing the amount of bits per pixel (I discussed this in Chapter 2). The goal, however, is to always maintain the fine balance of compression or bit-depth modification and visual quality. This is the key aspect of color retention.

The process of balancing reduction of file weight with retention of quality is the specific definition of optimization, and demands skill and a fine eye. Depending on the file format you use, compressing the file can compromise the quality of the final image. Ultimately, it's going to be up to you to determine where the best option lies. This is why it's so important to understand which formats and what features are available to you—and to have started with quality materials and techniques from which to process your finals.

There are also special considerations regarding each graphic file format. For example, GIFs can be transparent, interlaced, or used to create animations. JPEGs can be progressively rendered, and enjoy the distinction of using a compression method that does not reduce the number of colors in an image. How and when to use each of these types of files is critical to optimization.

PNG offers anti-aliasing and transparency features that are much more sophisticated than GIF and non-existent in JPEG

SWF, or "Flash" format for short, is a vector-based motion format for the Web. You can make SWF files with Flash, LiveMotion, and Corel10

SVG—Scalable Vector Graphics—use XML mark-up as their underlying technology, not binary data as in more traditional Web graphics

GIF

GIFs (pronounced either with a hard or soft "g") is the Graphic Interchange Format. It was developed in the late 1980s for Compuserve. The GIF is the oldest supported file format on the Web. GIFs are extremely popular because they are small and have considerable functionality such as animation, interlacing and transparency capabilities.

GIFs use a method of compression known as *Lossless*. This compression means that even though the file is compressed, it ideally does not lose any quality in the final image. Although the file size of a compressed, lossless image is smaller than an uncompressed file, the data remains true to the original file. Of course, the only way to obtain lossless results using GIF is to make good decisions about which kinds of images are best suited to the format.

The GIF file format only supports up to 256 colors. This is one of the disadvantages of using a GIF file to compress a photographic image. The thousands of colors that comprise a photograph are converted to a very limited number of colors, and you will in fact lose quality.

Therefore, the GIF format is recommended primarily for images that use less than 256 colors, or can be readily limited to 256 colors or less.

Good choices for compressing to GIF format include:

Any drawing with a few areas of flat color, such as found in this digital cell for an animation by Joe Forkan (Figure 3.4).

Line drawings. Forkan's clean lines and few areas of gray in this sample make it a perfect choice for GIF format (Figure 3.5).

Clip art (Figure 3.6).

3.4

A flat drawing with few areas of color—great for GIF format!

3.5

Clean line drawings with very few areas of gray are suitable for GIF format

3.6

Clip art. Again, simple color and clean lines are most effective for GIF files

3.7

A poorly suited image choice
for GIF

3.8

A poorly suited image
for GIF results in banding
and color problems

3.9

Example of a posterized photo

3.10

"Stigmata"—Using color
reduction in GIF to achieve
special effects

Further compression occurs during GIF processing when unnecessary colors are eliminated from an image. This is done by reducing the number of color channels in a process known as *indexing* color.

This process creates a specialized palette based on the colors in your file. When converting to indexed color, a Color Lookup table (CLUT) is built which stores the image's colors. If a color in the original image does not appear in the table, the program chooses the closest one or simulates the color using the CLUT colors. There are a number of palettes within the indexing process. In most widely used imaging programs such as Photoshop, each indexing process creates a different type of CLUT, as follows:

Perceptual
This palette creates a priority for those colors which impact human vision most intensely. Using this palette keeps colors as bright and diverse as possible to maintain the pre-compression integrity.

Selective
As with the perceptual palette, this option prioritizes colors in order of importance while attempting to adapt to the lowest number of colors possible.

Adaptive
This creates a palette by sampling the colors appearing most commonly in the image.

Web
The Web CLUT uses the palette most often used by Web browsers to display 8-bit images. This method uses a subset of the Mac or Windows System palette.

System (Mac)
This CLUT takes a uniform sample of RGB colors of the Mac system's default 8-bit palette.

Perceptual: This color table chooses from colors that are most readily perceived by the human eye

Selective: This palette prioritizes colors in order of importance while attempting to adapt to the lowest number of colors possible

Adaptive: The Adaptive color table uses the best colors based on the image

Web: This color table makes use of the Web-safe 216 colors only

System: This color table takes a uniform sample of RGB colors of the Macintosh system's default 8-bit palette

The Web color palette ensures that your images will be indexed to colors that are standard on both the Windows and Macintosh platform. You can see a sample of the Web-safe palette at: www.visibone.com/swatches/.

The number of colors chosen for a GIF is referred to as *Bit* or *Color Depth*. This term describes the number of bits of color information per pixel within an image. Bit depth determines the number of colors used to display or print an image. For example, if you choose 4 bits per pixel, the image will be composed of 16 colors; 6 bits per pixel, 64 colors; 8 bits per pixel, 256 colors. With GIFs, you can use a specific value up to a total 256. It's important to select a reasonable number of colors to manage your file properly.

An image with a bit depth that is too low will appear posterized (Figure 3.9). Sometimes this is desirable if you're going after a specific effect (Figure 3.10) such as the one I created for a digital photo on www.mike-forkan.com. Large areas of flat color will be adjacent to each other. The trick is to get the lowest bit depth while retaining the highest image quality for the application desired.

3.11

Reducing colors from left to right: 256 colors, 32 colors, 4 colors

Types of GIFs

One of the major advantages of the GIF format is that it offers three very important options that you'll want to take advantage of when exporting your graphics.

Interlaced GIFs are a specific file type which offer progressive rendering. Transparent GIFs allow portions of your graphic to be see-through. Animated GIFs enable you to create dynamic events contained within a single GIF file.

Interlaced GIFs

GIFs can be interlaced to appear progressively on the screen. The image first appears in a rudimentary manner and details are filled in as the file continues to load. This allows visitors to get an idea of what is about to appear, and can choose to continue navigating or to wait for the completed image. Most broadband users won't even notice progressive rendering on any Web graphic that is optimized for modems.

Interlaced GIFs are useful for design elements that are not critical to the use or readability of your site. Elements such as navigation bars should not be interlaced because visitors need to see the entire navigation bar in order to utilize your site. It is also not recommended that you interlace GIFs used for backgrounds.

Transparent GIFs

Another important aspect of the GIF format is that areas of it can be made transparent. This means you can make an illustration or object appear to be free-form against a background, blending with rather than being separated from the background design.

Animated GIFs

Due to a looping mechanism within GIF technology, we are able to create multiple images and combine them into a single file. This results in the very popular animated GIF.

Animated GIFs tend to be fast-loading, yet they offer movement to otherwise static Web pages. You can make animated GIFs using numerous tools such as LiveMotion, Fireworks, Flash, and so on. There are also some very good shareware applications on the market.

There are several general terms you'll need to know. These will vary depending upon your application and application version.

Note: Users of Photoshop versions 5 and up can use the very helpful Save for Web feature.

Helpful terms include:

Indexing
A software program such as Photoshop will take an image file and count its colors. If there are more than 256 colors in an image, indexing will reduce the palette to 256 colors. At that point, you have the freedom to determine if further reduction in colors is appropriate.

Palette Type
There are several types of indexed color palettes. The one that is most important to you is going to be the *adaptive* color palette. This palette allows you to determine the various aspects of the palette, such as color depth and dithering. Another important palette is the *exact* palette. You'll see this appear when an image already has less than 256 colors.

Color Depth
This is also referred to as "bit" depth. This is basically the amount of data that will be saved with your image. Optimization of GIFs largely depends upon your ability to reduce bit depth.

Number of Colors
This is the total number of colors in the image, which can begin as low as 8 and end up as high as 256. Limiting colors is helpful in terms of reducing total file size. Typically, you'll only need to worry about managing your color depth, and the number of colors will reduce appropriately.

Dithering
Dithering is the process of allowing the computer to make decisions as to what colors to put into an image. For example, if you have three yellows next to one another, the computer may select the yellow that is in its own palette. This means that your pastel could end up as a neon! You can control how much your colors dither in Photoshop, but ideally, you will not want any dithering at all.

The acronym JPEG (pronounced jay-peg) stands for Joint Experts Photographic Group, the name of the organization that originally wrote the compression algorithm for this file type. JPEGs are extremely efficient at compressing a variety of designs.

Unlike GIF, which uses lossless compression and a limited color palette, JPEGs use *Lossy* compression and 24-bit color (millions of colors). JPEG compression removes what it considers irrelevant data from the file to compress the data. While this loss in data is sometimes invisible to the naked eye, there are instances where the compression is very noticeable. As with GIFs, your understanding of which images are suitable for optimization with the JPEG format will help ensure the end quality of the graphics you save to this format.

Art that is suitable for JPEG compression includes:

Photographs
Any photograph is suitable for the JPEG format. This is especially true of photographs with natural gradations of color, such as are found in sunsets, sky views, and views of water (Figure 3.12).

Gradient designs
If you're using a color gradient, the JPEG option can help you keep the subtle changes in color intact. Many times, GIF format will cause these colors to break up, creating an effect referred to as banding (Figure 3.13).

Illustrations with many colors
If you have a very detailed illustration with colors and shadows, JPEG will offer better compression than GIF (Figure 3.14).

Complex designs
Any design or photo that has a combination of gradient, light source, colors, and any other digital data is likely to be well-suited for the JPEG format (Figure 3.15).

3.12
Dramatic sky and
bright color can be retained
best in JPEG format

3.14
Forkan's political illustration
for the Tucson Weekly has
variegated color which is best
suited to JPEGs

3.15
Complex designs are also
best suited to JPEG.
The compression maintains
more highlight, light gradients,
and fine detail

3.13

JPEG retains color

3.13

GIF format causes banding

Progressive JPEGs

When a JPEG is loaded on the Web, the compressed data produces a generalized calculation of how the image should appear. JPEG files can produce truly extraordinary compression, but the more you compress the file, the more data is removed from the calculations. This can cause areas of the image to appear blocky or leave trace halos (called artifacts) around portions of the image (Figure 3.17). It is important, therefore, to compress your image carefully and balance the loss of quality against the decreased file size.

You can control the quality of a JPEG image in a variety of ways depending upon your imaging program. The quality control affects the amount of compression. Higher qualities yield lower compression but retain more of the original quality of the image.

Interestingly, JPEGs can render progressively, although they use a different technology than is found in GIF. I've always said that progressive JPEGs look as though they've got Vaseline smeared on them. The initial images are very blurry, but after several passes, the image becomes clear.

3.16

A well-compressed JPEG

3.17

Poor compression leads to
compression artifacts

Optimizing JPEGs

PNG

JPEG compression in Photoshop has the following settings of concern to the Web designer:

Maximum
This is the highest setting, and maintains as much of the file's integrity as possible.

High
Still a good choice, some lossy compression occurs at this level.

Medium
Lossy compression really goes to work here, reducing the file size even more—but often at a noticeable degradation to the image's integrity.

Low
At this level, most JPEGs are unacceptable in my opinion, as the appearance of artifacts becomes very noticeable. This setting should be avoided unless you are able to maintain the image's strength without encountering serious problems with clarity.

The Portable Network Graphics (PNG) format was introduced as an alternative to the GIF format. PNG supports 24-bit images and has transparency capabilities with anti-aliasing, which allows for smooth lines.

As with GIF, PNG is a lossless compression method, meaning that quality should not suffer as the image is compressed. Unlike GIF or JPEG, however, PNG supports many different bit depths and storage methods. This makes PNG extremely flexible.

As with GIF, PNG can support RGB and grayscale images with one alpha channel as a transparency mask. PNG can also support Bitmap and indexed-color modes without alpha channels. PNG uses the saved alpha channel to define transparency in the file.

PNG is supported by Internet Explorer 4.0 (IE) and above. This makes it a risky choice for Web use right now. Many people feel PNG holds promise for the future, however, so it is worth study.

3.18
Viewing a well-compressed PNG file in IE. High quality, low file size, but unfortunately, poor browser support

Down to Basics

So what it boils down to when it comes to color and Web graphics is a simple two-step process in general:

Examine the image.

Choose the best file type for the desired quality retention.

It's actually very impressive what today's Web graphic production tools can do. This is especially true of Adobe and Macromedia products, but many smaller companies have done admirable work in the creation of imaging software for the Web. Look around and give everything a try.

Next Along the Wheel

Producing great color via Web graphics does take a fine touch. This means you'll have to practice a range of techniques, including those learned in this chapter. But the results will be worth it!

Next up is a look at color, psychology, gender, and culture. If that sounds like a college course, well, it should be! It's a fascinating study, and one that I'm certain will have impact on you both as an interested reader and a student of Web design.

COLOR DESIGN FOR A GLOBAL ENVIRONMENT

Chapter Four

Whether a site visitor knows it or not, he or she responds to visual cues on a psychological level. Well-educated graphic designers have been taught how to strategically create and place such cues to tease, please, and ultimately satisfy their visitors. And the satisfaction doesn't end with the visitor, of course. A happy site visitor is more likely to engage in the goal of your site—whether it is meant to inform, entertain, or to sell goods or services.

Did you know that a site visitor has formed his or her first impression of your site within the first nine seconds of a visit? So how in the world—taking download time into account—do designers effectively entice and satisfy visitors? The answer is simple: appropriate design.

In basic terms, appropriate design is the act of matching the demographics and content of your website to specifically chosen colors and other design styles. This ensures that the combination of visual elements adds up to a design that's suitable to the content, and fits the audience with no need for additional tailoring.

The most obvious way to work on a visitor's psyche is to use color as a means of conveying messages about the site and its information or products. Color is surprisingly an often overlooked design element! But, it is also extremely powerful in what it represents, how it's combined with other elements, and the way it expresses information on a subtle level.

This chapter will look specifically at color from a psychological perspective, and help you apply each with forethought and intention to provide your audiences with the best possible user experience.

A visual stimulus, such as color, will elicit an emotional response.

Color Choice

Gallery: Basic Color Symbolism

Color choice is paramount in eliciting an appropriate visual response from visitors. Color is one of the first things your audience sees, and you can set up your pages so that color appears immediately. This quickly sets the tone for the entire site experience.

To achieve effective color design, begin by selecting colors that express your site's intent. The palette that you develop must match the site's personality and goals.

If you're representing a community website, for example, you'll typically want to choose warm colors to create a sense of comfort and ease. If your site is meant to be informative, with the words carrying most of the weight, the site colors should be simple and not distracting.

In order to best grasp the complex nature of color symbolism, I'll take you on a tour of basic colors and color meanings.

The following gallery of general color themes will help you get started understanding the symbolism of color—as well as the oft-times paradoxical nature of that symbolism.

The gallery also serves to help you understand the general psychological relationship between colors and people. Because, as a Web designer, not only must your color palette match the site content, but you should choose colors that reflect your audience's values.

Running along the top of each page are some cultural quirks associated with the various colors shown. This too acts as a general guide for choosing to use, or not to use, a particular color for your audiences.

GAY.COM

home   channels   people   shop   search   my Gay.com

chat | homepages | member profiles | message boards | volunteers

People

Start planning!

pride

Communities
Activist Way
Bisexual
Leather
Transgender
Women
Youth

Gay.com Pics

Photo album
Women's pics

Interact
Go chat
Build homepages
Add chat to a site
Post messages
Chat guidelines
Volunteer

Look who's supporting Gay.com!

Sitemap
Help

abuzz

Today's Features

IN MESSAGE BOARDS
Are you a proud lesbian, bi or transgender mom? Then we want you! Send photos of you and your kids to photoalbum@gay.com for our Mother's Day photo album, and help us show the world what our families look like!

VOLUNTEER OF THE WEEK
For Spike, boards monitor "gives new meaning to the statement 'We're Everywhere!' As a butch who's seen hir share of negative stereotyping take its toll, it's rewarding to have a forum to speak out and to enlighten our own community to who we really are." View her profile or find her in the message boards!

Interact

Visit the Boards:
Our community's talking about everything from coming-out support and political debates to celebrity worship and gossip fests.

Hot threads:
- Why be bi?
- Long distance love
- Gender 101
- The Sapphic Seer

Member Profiles
View a profile: Search by Gay.com member name.
E-mail us: Want your profile featured here?
Edit your profile: Add photos or personal secrets!

Featured profiles:
ponyboy69, DickDandy, Yinzara, Ryanboy29, MichaelfromNYC, IndoGurl-NYC, smokeeater2u, BaltoButch, Sir-Krusha, Schatzy

In Chat
Chat room list: Find the room that's right for you.
Add chat to your site: Become a Gay.com affiliate.

Build a homepage!
Create your own homepage—it's free, easy and fun.
Featured homepages:
PARTY: With the Gay.com Illinois chat room
MEET: Sexy cowboy bartenders at a Nashville gay bar
Search Gay.com member's homepages!

Top 10 featured GLBT books

insightoutbooks.com

Join: Get 3 books for $3
Click for details
1. Losing Matt Shepard
2. 101 Survival Secrets
3. Lesbian Film Guide
4. Stitching a Revolution
5. A Density of Souls
6. The Well of Loneliness
7. The Coming Storm
8. Sir Elton
9. Front Runner
10. The Night Listener
List provided by insightoutbooks.com

Style Picks

Che Guevara Sleeveless Tee
For the bad ass punk inside of you.
Get It!

Animated E-shirt
Light up the dance floor. Literally.
Get It!

Women we love

Joan says: "Dykes Rule"
Find out about punk rock girl Joan Jett's "Bad Reputation."
- Amy Ray goes "Stag"
- Comedian Suzanne Westenhoefer
- Indie star Ani DiFranco
- Artist Alison Bechdel

Global Gay.com   fr.gay.com   latino.gay.com   uk.gay.com   port.gay.com   gay.it

Home   Channels   People   Shop   Search   my Gay.com   Chat   Sitemap   Help

Company info   Advertising info   Jobs available   Privacy policy   Site terms   Contact us

4.1

Gay.com community site: orange for warmth, purple for Gay pride

> **RED**

In China, a symbol of celebration and good luck.

power

energy

love

warmth

passion

aggression

danger

> **BLUE**

Color of immortality in China, holiness for the Jews, color of Krishna in Hinduism. Blue is the safest global color.

trust

conservative

security

technology

cleanliness

sorrow

order

> **GREEN**

Green tends to be calming and antidepressant. It is associated with money in the U.S., but not in many other cultures.

nature
earth
health
good luck
jealousy
renewal
money

YELLOW

Sacred and imperial color in Asian cultures, represents joy and happiness in several Western cultures. Women tend to respond quite positively to many values of yellow.

optimism

hope

philosophy

dishonesty

cowardice

betrayal

> PURPLE

Purple is associated with mourning or New-Age and alternative
religions in some cultures. Should be avoided in many instances.
Interestingly, purple is rarely found in nature.

spirituality

mystery

royalty

power

transformation

cruelty

arrogance

homosexuality

> ORANGE

Symbolizes that a product is inexpensive in the U.S., so it should be avoided when designing sites that are expressing sophistication, elegance, and luxury.

energy

balance

warmth

> BROWN

Brown is usually quite neutral and associated with nature.

earth

reliability

comfort

endurance

> GRAY

Grey is widely used as a neutralizing colour. Silver tones express sophistication.

intellect

futurism

elegance (silver tones)

modesty

sadness

decay

> WHITE

Salvation, holiness, purity in most Western and many world cultures, but mourning in some Western and many Eastern cultures. Should be used with care in certain instances. Because white is such a necessary color for contrast and design, it's wise to mix it with another color that has stronger, more obvious significance.

purity

cleanliness

precision

innocence

sterility

death

BLACK

Represents mourning in many cultures, also evil, and dark spirits. Paradoxically, black is seen as sophisticated and elegant, especially in cosmopolitan, prosperous areas.

power

sexuality

sophistication

mystery

fear

unhappiness

death

International Colors

The Impact of Color and Culture

Some fascinating studies exist about how people around the world respond and react to color. The color orange, for example, represents goods that are inexpensive—except on Halloween and St. Patrick's Day! In the U.S., blue is a color that represents trust. However, in Korea, trust is gained visually via pastels —especially pink. An understanding of what colors represent to your demographic will help you design a site that will appeal to your audience.

The way color is used in a worldwide context is a profound issue that is often misunderstood or overlooked by Web designers. How it's used on the screen is made more challenging by the fact that the perception of color depends not only upon our ability to see that color, but also on our ability to interpret it within the context of our emotional and cultural realities.

Color can entice, frighten, persuade, sell, and even inspire. I've often pointed out that our job as Web designers is to use color effectively to present our art, information, product, service, or organization. If we're attempting to convey our message to a global audience, we must do so with an awareness of color's cultural significance.

To demonstrate the impact of color and culture, let me remind you of a fashion trend that occurred in the '90s. Suddenly, it became popular for brides in the U.S. to use black garments in their wedding parties. Those brave souls undoubtedly shocked and disturbed members of their families!

A woman from Thailand and I had quite a laugh realizing that if we were to wear black wedding gowns or have black anywhere in our weddings, both of our mothers (mine is of the Jewish variety) would be mortified. The connotations for both of our cultures are far too charged with symbols of unhappiness, bad luck, and even evil.

Why were brides of a more contemporary generation choosing to use black in their bridal pageants? Well, along with all the negative connotations, black is also seen as very elegant and cosmopolitan. It is also antiestablishment, suggesting personal rather than community power. So, in some very unsubtle ways, U.S. brides who chose to use black rather than white were making a statement regarding their sophistication and personal strength—two concepts the final decade of 20th-century American culture completely embodied.

To get some help and insight on how complexities of color can be tamed by Web designers seeking to create strong relationships with their site visitors, I turned to Jill Morton, an author, designer, and professor at the University of Hawaii. Morton is considered one of few world experts on color, and has done studies regarding color in advertising design and on the Web. She affirms my oft-voiced perspective that audience is paramount. "Do your homework, know your target market," she corroborates. "Total global accessibility is a real challenge."

If you're designing for a worldwide audience, note that blue is the most globally accessible color. "Blue happens to be one of the colors that is safe in almost every culture," Morton says. As a result, you can use blue for just about any kind of site, regardless of its audience, goal, or location. But why is blue so globally attractive? Morton speculates that "there's nothing on the planet that exists in isolation except the sky— that stands alone." She notes that in most religions, "the deity is above. The nasty thing is down below, in the dark."

Some colors fall into vague categories. Pink is one such example. "If you're designing for an East Indian audience," advises Morton, "get rid of pale pink." Many East Indian men feel that pink is a feminine color. But in other countries, such as Japan, pastels are very popular with both sexes.

One color is particularly unsafe in a global environment—purple. Purple, according to Morton, is a "polarizing color...it is potentially hazardous on a global level." In Catholic Europe, purple is a symbol of death and crucifixion. I have heard anecdotally that in some Middle Eastern cultures purple signifies prostitution, much as red is used in some Western countries, as in a "Red Light District." Purple is also symbolic of mysticism and spiritual beliefs that go against Christian, Jewish, and Muslim paradigms: Wicca, New Age spirituality, homosexuality, and

paganism. A case in point is the launch of Euro Disney. The first design for signs used large amounts of purple, which visitors found "morbid." This response was completely contradictory to the happy message that Disney wanted to convey. As a result, Disney had to rework its European advertising campaign, which doubtlessly wound up costing significant money and time.

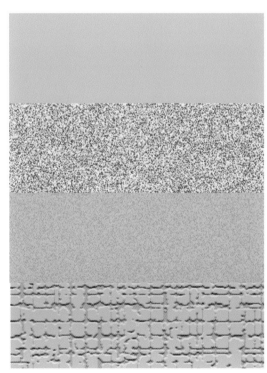

4.2

Texture changes color

4.3

IBM: "Big Blue" conveys a
conservative look

Microsoft

All Products

Home | Events/Training | Subscribe | About Microsoft | US/Worldwide | Downloads | Contact Us | MSN.com

Search

[_____] GO

Product Family Sites
Windows
Office
Servers
Developer Tools

Web Services
Office eServices
Windows Update
MSN
bCentral

Customer Sites
Home & Personal
Business
IT Professional
Developer
Partner/Reseller
Education

Resources
Order Microsoft Products
Microsoft Press Books
Media Information
Newsletters
Microsoft Jobs
Privacy Statement
Freedom to Innovate
Support

Celebrate Clippy's demise!
Attend the Office XP launch in your city to see why Clippy's out of a job. You'll get a $100 Office XP rebate coupon, software, and more. ⊕

U.S. only.

Exchange 5.5 to Exchange 2000: Find practical, technical guidance on upgrading.

How H&R Block gave its overtaxed servers some relief.

Virtual Private Networking. Securely connect remote users to your network over the Internet.

Microsoft Office XP

Try Office XP. Time-saving features such as Smart Tags must be experienced to be believed. U.S. and Canada only.

Today's News ▲

• Pre-order Office XP for launch day and get free shipping. U.S. only.

• Be among the first to get Microsoft Visual Studio.NET Beta 2 by attending Tech·Ed.

• Windows XP at home: See how you'll get a lot more from your PC.

More News ⊕

New Downloads ▲

• Internet Explorer 6 Preview Edition offers new integrated messaging and privacy features.

• Windows 2000 SP1 has the latest in compatibility, setup, reliability, and security updates.

More Downloads ⊕

Last Updated: Monday, April 30, 2001 - 4:42 p.m. Pacific Time
©2001 Microsoft Corporation. All rights reserved. Terms of Use
Text-only Home Page | Disability/accessibility | Contact Us | Privacy Statement

4.4

Microsoft: safely global

閲覧　出品　各種サービス　検索　ヘルプ　コミュニティー

世界のオークションコミュニティ

カテゴリー

アンティーク・アート
おもちゃ・ゲーム
コレクション
コンピュータ・周辺機器
ジュエリー・アクセサリー

チケット・旅行
電化製品・カメラ
ファッション・ブランド
本・映画・音楽
その他の品物
全てのカテゴリ...

世界のイーベイ

eBay.com
オーストラリア
オーストリア
カナダ
フランス
ドイツ
イタリア
アイルランド
ニュージーランド
スイス
イギリス

イーベイジャパン内検索

検索　ヒント

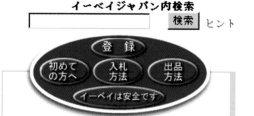

登録
初めての方へ　入札方法　出品方法
イーベイは安全です

特選アイテム

☆★Tommy Hilfiger★☆SheerタンクトップBlue
デジカメ Olympus C-990
★コンビニ限定チョロQ★日産エスカルゴ★
ライカコピ-!ニッカ3-Sレンジファインダ-
シャーリーテンプル女児サンドレス
サンリオSF文庫 死の迷宮
全ての特選アイテム

イーベイジャパンのおすすめ

更新日時：05月01日　23時18分58秒　日本時間

お知らせ

100%
無料です!

話題のコーナー

コンピューター・ハード＆ソフトウェア、ゲーム

ブランド グッチ シャネル フェンディ

アフィリエート プログラム 開始 NEW!

売り手も買い手も安心です

イーベイモバイル 移動中でも入札できます。

It's important to remember that colors change depending upon how we as designers apply them. Three issues that alter color are texture, the amount of color in use, and juxtaposition with other colors.

When a designer applies a texture to a color, that color changes (Figure 4.2). Smooth surfaces make a color appear lighter, and rough surfaces make a color appear darker. So if you're using cyan, but adding rough texture, the color may veer more toward blue in the context of global audiences.

Similarly, different amounts of color create different effects. A little bit of purple in an international design might be fine, but lots of it may cause the problems mentioned earlier. Also, the balance of different colors in the same design requires a fine eye—which color dominates? That's the color you need to think about the most in terms of global cultures.

Even more important is mixing colors, which can completely change meanings. If we revisit the bride scenario, we find that white, which many Western and some Eastern cultures consider a symbol of purity and cleanliness, is considered bad luck in China and Japan, where it's the color of mourning. The same is true in India, where a bride in all white would foreshadow unhappiness. But if you mix these colors with others, such as red, the significance changes and the negative connotations are lessened or eliminated.

In fact, red—especially in China—is a symbol of luck. As a result, it makes sense if you're attracting Chinese visitors to use lots of red in your design. When combined with white, the red becomes even more powerful, and the white is neutralized.

Another issue often missed when determining color is gender. Men's and women's reactions to color are significantly different and, when combined with cultural issues, the challenge becomes quite complex.

"In our culture, real men don't eat quiche and they don't use color terms like 'mauve' and 'teal,'" quips Morton. "I don't think men are as sensitive as women to color."

The Meaning of Color for Gender by Natalia Khouw points out some interesting theories derived from academic studies about color and gender, including the following:

Blue stands out for men much more than for women.

Men prefer blue to red, women red to blue.

Men prefer orange to yellow, women yellow to orange.

Women's color tastes are thought to be more diverse than men's.

One of the studies cited in the paper was done in Nepal, where men and women were asked to list all of the colors they could think of. Women were able to consistently list more colors than men could. A similar study in England had parallel results, with women identifying many more colors than men could.

While it's difficult to make assumptions about research of this nature, it's interesting to look at color and gender in the context of a given culture. More importantly, that gender plays a role in the perception of color indicates that to communicate effectively Web designers must know their audience as well as possible.

Color for Web Designers

With these issues in mind, it becomes obvious that we have to spend time evaluating our approach to a given visual design. Currently, most designers don't think about color and culture.

Morton says that "90 per cent of the Web uses color poorly. It's overdone. There's no sense of color harmony." Part of the problem, she feels, is that people with no design background get involved, and get really enthusiastic. Enthusiasm can lead to overuse of color in inappropriate venues. What's more, people without design backgrounds have a fatal tendency to want to design for themselves rather than for their audience.

Clients of more experienced visual designers often do the same thing. They get excited and want to design to their own tastes rather than what makes sense for their potential visitors.

Whether you're a newcomer to visual design or an experienced designer, you can benefit from thinking about some basic approaches to global visual design. "The first rule is to take that particular product and service and find a color naturally associated with it," recommends Morton. "Let's say the site is about healthy food. There are certain colors that are associated with natural food. [If it's] firecrackers— you'd choose something associated with fire, such as red."

Natural associations tend to be pretty safe. Just don't make ethnocentric assumptions about associations. In the U.S., all paper money is green. We have the most boring and ugly money around, although it's extremely easy to identify! Other countries use multiple colors in their paper money design. So, while green might be a fine color for a finance site servicing U.S.-only customers, it might be entirely incorrect for this context in another country.

Globalization of Color

An interesting phenomenon, which may be partially due to the Web's proliferation throughout the world, is that some of the cultural connotations of color are becoming less intense for younger generations—particularly as they become more influenced by U.S. commercial interests.

Despite this concern, if you're designing for international audiences, remember that how you use color to represent your product or information has a significant impact on how it will be received. Designers should feel good about the use of color, and be assertive in how it's used. But you must also think carefully about why you're using a given color or selection of colors, and to whom that color is being delivered. Without forethought, the results could weaken your color message—or worse, make it ineffective altogether.

Books

The Art and Science of Web Design,
      Veen, Jeffrey.
      New Riders Publishing.
      Indianapolis, Indiana, U.S.A.
      ISBN 0-7897-2370-0

Color Harmony: A Guide to Creative
      Color Combinations,
      Chijiiwa, Hideaki.
      Rockport Publishers,
      Rockport, Massachusetts, U.S.A.
      ISBN 0-935603-06-9

Graphic Design School,
      Swann, Alan.
      Van Nostrand Reinhold,
      New York, New York, U.S.A.
      ISBN 0-442-30423-4

Principles of Color,
      Birren, Faber.
      Schiffer Publishing, Pennsylvania,
      U.S.A.
      ISBN 0-88740-103-1

Principles of Color Design:
      Designing with Electronic Color,
      Wong, Wucius.
      Van Nostrand Reinhold,
      New York, New York, U.S.A.
      ISBN 0-442-02067-8

Websites

Color Matters: Online work of color expert
      J. L. Morton. A fascinating
      repository of information on color
      including electronic color guide-
      books for designers:
      http://www.colormatters.com/

Online portfolio of the illustration,
      cartooning, and painting
      of Joe Forkan:
      http://www.joeforkan.com/

Online portfolio of the landscape,
      portraiture, and digital imagery
      of Derrick Story:
      http://www.storyphoto.com/

Tucson Weekly:
      http://www.tucsonweekly.com/

Visibone color references for
      Web designers:
      http://www.visibone.com/

Death of the Web-safe Color Palette
      by David Lehn and Hadley Stern
      in Webmonkey:
      http://hotwired.lycos.com/
      webmonkey/00/37/index2a.html

WebMonkey Web Developer's Resource:
      http://www.webmonkey.com/

Web Standards Project:
      http://www.webstandards.org/

Coalition of Web developers and users
      encouraging Web standards.